KITCHENER'S LAST VOLUNTEER

KITCHENER'S LAST VOLUNTEER

The Life of Henry Allingham, the Oldest Surviving Veteran of the Great War

HENRY ALLINGHAM
WITH DENNIS GOODWIN

MAINSTREAM
PUBLISHING

EDINBURGH AND LONDON

First published in Great Britain in 2008 by
MAINSTREAM PUBLISHING COMPANY
(EDINBURGH) LTD
7 Albany Street
Edinburgh EH1 3UG

ISBN 9781845964160

A catalogue record for this book is available
from the British Library

Typeset in Disintegration and Garamond

Printed in Great Britain by
Clays Ltd, St Ives plc

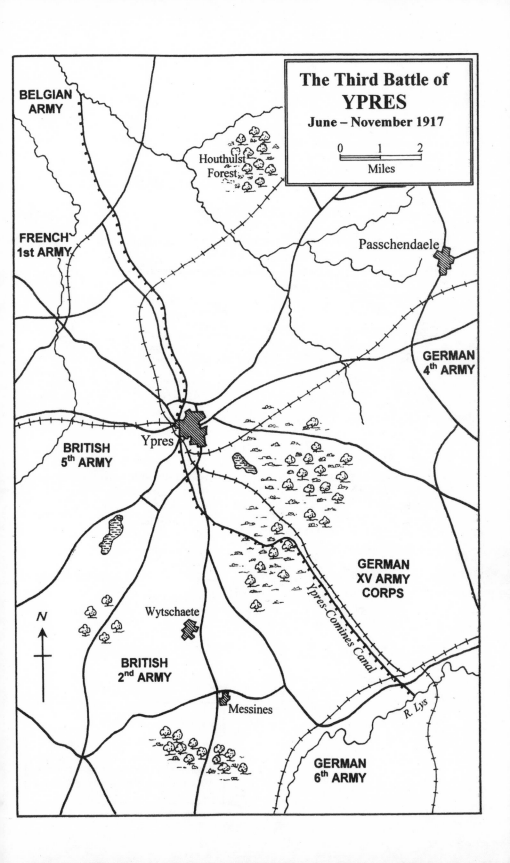

The Third Battle of
YPRES
June – November 1917

0   1   2
Miles

BELGIAN
ARMY

Houthulst
Forest

Passchendaele

FRENCH
1st ARMY

GERMAN
4th ARMY

BRITISH
5th ARMY

Ypres

N

GERMAN
XV ARMY
CORPS

Wytschaete

Ypres-Comines Canal

BRITISH
2nd ARMY

Messines

R. Lys

GERMAN
6th ARMY

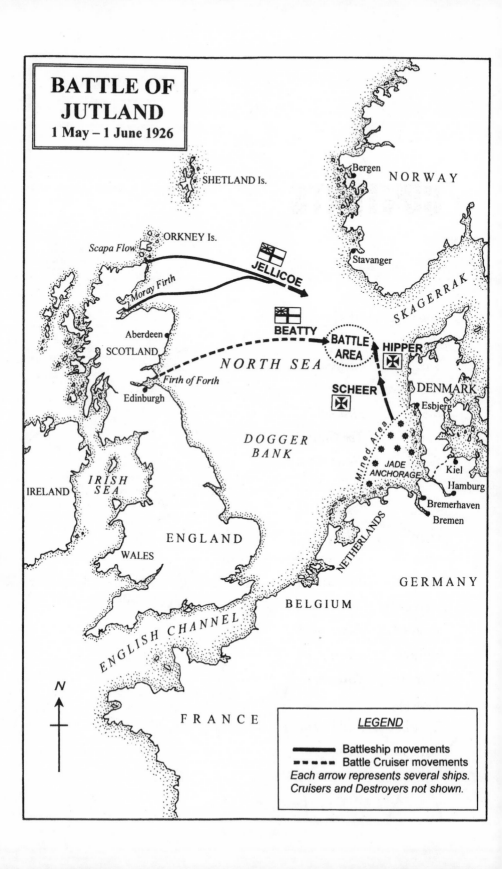

BATTLE OF JUTLAND
1 May – 1 June 1926

NORWAY

Bergen

SHETLAND Is.

Stavanger

ORKNEY Is.

Scapa Flow

SKAGERRAK

JELLICOE

Moray Firth

BEATTY

BATTLE AREA

HIPPER

Aberdeen

SCOTLAND

NORTH SEA

SCHEER

DENMARK

Firth of Forth

Esbjerg

Edinburgh

Mined Area

DOGGER BANK

JADE ANCHORAGE

Kiel

IRISH SEA

Hamburg

IRELAND

Bremerhaven

Bremen

ENGLAND

NETHERLANDS

WALES

GERMANY

BELGIUM

ENGLISH CHANNEL

N

FRANCE

LEGEND

——— Battleship movements
– – – Battle Cruiser movements
Each arrow represents several ships.
Cruisers and Destroyers not shown.

CONTENTS

FOREWORD

HENRY ALLINGHAM, WHO TURNED 112 years of age in June 2008, is one of our nation's historic treasures. His life has encapsulated mankind's prolific and speedy acceleration into the modern era as we know it. Henry was born before the age of modern politics, transport, communication, healthcare, monetary systems, the media and, of course, global consumerism that drives our lives today. One could argue the Edwardian age was something to look back on with fondness, but of course society has improved beyond all measure in how we care for ourselves and our neighbours.

It was a vastly different world that went down the road of calamitous conflict in 1914. At home there were privations aplenty and customs that we now think of as quaint. Overseas the mud of Flanders was stained with blood from soldiers thrown into a mire of madness. Only the fortunate survived and every home was touched by grief. Today we are lucky indeed that most of us do not have to make such stark choices nor suffer such a high price for them.

In the Great War, Henry volunteered, along with hundreds of thousands of others, and it is now remarkable that he is virtually the only one left alive to recall those momentous events. He fought on land, sea and in the air for his country; he is the last survivor of the Battle of Jutland in 1916, a survivor of the Battle of Ypres in 1917, and the sole survivor of the original RAF. He lost many comrades in combat and nearly died himself on the Western Front, yet he lived to tell the tale while millions perished. His story is vital to our understanding of life at that time in those dire circumstances that are now poised to drift into the dark shadows of time, and we should never forget the sacrifices made on our behalf.

Knowing Henry as I do, having met with him several times, I am fully aware of the highly significant work he carries out with the World War One Veterans' Association, telling his story to thousands of young people each year. He does not want modern society to forget what his generation gave for our futures, but equally, the message of peace and reconciliation is one that he desires to convey above all else.

Henry Allingham is a living piece of our British history, a link to our past whom we should cherish while he is still alive and able to re-tell his astonishing story. He has witnessed so much of our history including the sinking of the *Titanic*, the Great War, the Depression, the Second World War and the building of the Welfare State – taking in six of my forebears, as well as 21 prime ministers. This is a staggering achievement but, rather than sit on his laurels, and even at his age in life, Henry still wants to meet today's young people and tell his story. We should all be humbled by this quiet, genial man and his desire to extol peace and friendship to the world, despite all the horrors he witnessed at such a young and impressionable age.

I was very pleased to be asked by Dennis Goodwin of the World War One Veterans' Association to contribute to this remarkable man's autobiography. I would like to pay a special tribute to him, and through him, the many millions of men who served and died for their country in the Great War.

HRH Prince Charles

PREFACE

ON 6 JUNE 1896 Henry Allingham – or 'Young Harry', as he would be known – was born in the upstairs bedroom of a house in Eden Terrace, Harrington Hill, Upper Clapton, London. Once a village, Clapton – run through by the lively River Lea – was now a suburb of the capital served by city trams and with its own railway station, opened in 1872. Eden Terrace wasn't a grand neighbourhood but nor was it the realm of the dirt poor who inhabited large tracts of east London at the time.

Harry's mother, Amy, aged 22, was in the care of her own mother, Eleanora Foster, better known as Nellie, during her labour. Meanwhile his father, 26-year-old Henry Thomas Allingham, was waiting anxiously downstairs. Usually he worked on a Saturday as a mercantile clerk in his brother Dick's ironmongery business. But this Saturday he was nervously waiting for news about his first-born. He and Amy had been married on 25 September 1895 at Clapton Parish Church and were now about to become parents of a honeymoon baby. And what of the world that baby Harry was about to enter?

Queen Victoria was on the throne. Indeed, in 1896 she became Britain's longest-serving monarch after passing the benchmark set by her grandfather, George III. Her Golden Jubilee was already a distant memory. Aged 75, she reigned over a quarter of the globe as the British Empire was at its zenith.

Lord Salisbury was the Conservative prime minister. Sherlock Holmes, the fictional detective created by Sir Arthur Conan Doyle, was appearing in novels and in newspaper serials. The first movies were being screened in London, New York and Paris.

Harry was born in the same month as Jean Peugeot, the French car manufacturer. The same year also saw the births of writer F. Scott Fitzgerald (who died in 1940), lyricist Ira Gershwin (died 1983), Wallis Simpson, the controversial mistress of King Edward VIII (she died in 1986), and actor George Burns (died 1996). Alfred Nobel died in 1896 at the age of 63 – he invented dynamite and later used his large fortune to reward innovation in physics, chemistry, literature, medicine and peace in a prize scheme that still exists today. This was also the year of the first car accident fatality. Mrs Bridget Driscoll of Old Town, Croydon, was run over by a Roger-Benz car at Crystal Palace, London, on 17 August.

Six months before Henry was born, X-ray machines were invented. Soon afterwards, the first modern Olympic Games took place in Athens and featured wrestling, cycling, weightlifting and tennis among other sports. In the same year the *Daily Mail* was launched by Lord Northcliffe, with the lower social orders its target market.

On the day of his birth, *The Times*, priced at threepence, had its first five pages covered entirely by columns of advertisements. Among them was one for the Britannia Motor Carriage Company, offering shares to buyers. Company objectives, the advert claimed, were to take part in the development of the new horseless carriage industry and to acquire the patent rights for

Britannia motors, which ran 60 to 100 miles continuously at a maximum speed of 15 mph.

The year 1896 saw the first person in Britain fined for speeding. Walter Arnold was driving through Paddock Wood in Kent at 8 mph – four times the 2 mph limit imposed on built-up areas by the Locomotive Act 1865 – when he was spotted by a local constable who was having his lunch in a nearby cottage. The constable donned a police helmet and chased the car on his bicycle. He eventually apprehended Mr Arnold, who was later fined one shilling. There were just 20 cars in Britain at the time.

A letter inside *The Times* revealed the plight of a private in the Coldstream Guards whose wife had died and left him with three children aged six, four and two. The father could afford only three shillings and sixpence, enough to support just one child. According to the Queen's Regulations, this meant that two of his children would have to find a charity to finance their expenses or face going to the workhouse. The letter, sent by the secretary of the Church of England's Waifs and Strays Society, asked that more cash be found from army funds to meet the costs of children of serving soldiers.

The newspaper also reported on an expeditionary force being sent to the Sudan. Horatio Herbert Kitchener, a man who would later play a pivotal role in Henry's life, was in action there, endorsing British rule in the heart of Africa. Although benevolent, the British occupation was against the will of most Sudanese people. The sports pages described how the Australian touring side, all amateurs, were getting the better of Gloucester, a long-standing cricket team featuring the legendary W.G. Grace.

As baby Harry was delivered just before midday, weighing 7 lb 4 oz, no one could have predicted the colourful future that lay ahead of him. Tragedy lurked in the wings. His father died just three years later, aged 29, while his mother succumbed to cancer aged 41. Their deaths occurred at a time when life expectancy for men stood at 45 and for women, 48.

And as a young man, Henry witnessed at close quarters one of the greatest disasters to befall mankind. The First World War claimed at least 15 million lives. About a third of Allied casualties occurred in the trenches, the corridor bunkers that housed soldiers during the conflict's long-running stalemates. It wasn't only enemy action that soldiers feared. There were rampant brown and black rats, nits, lice, trench fever and trench foot. Poor weather also caused trench subsidence. Assaults on the senses sometimes brought about mental, as well as physical, collapse.

As an aircraft mechanic for the Royal Naval Air Service (RNAS), Henry was not directly involved in trench warfare but he is in no doubt that it was the men who served in these hellholes who won the war. He was also one of the founder members of the Royal Air Force (RAF) in 1918. Later he witnessed the effects of the Second World War from the home front, where he helped to research technological advances negating the Nazi use of magnetic mines on our ports and harbours that helped keep the British Isles safe.

After the war Henry watched the world transform with the arrival of computers, the jet engine and airline travel, the National Health Service, terrorism, nuclear warfare, television and telecommunications. The age of the motorcar and the movie has unfolded during his lifetime. Since his birth the world has said farewell to polio, scurvy and smallpox and beckoned in penicillin, contraceptive drugs and AIDS. The Cold War, the space race and Concorde have come and gone. And perhaps no one is more surprised than Henry to find that he is now a celebrity. He consorts with royalty and prime ministers at state functions. He travels across Britain and Europe to keep alive the memory of men who perished in the First World War and teach the younger generation to respect life and one another.

But it wasn't always like this. Once, not so long ago, Henry led a life that was unremarkable and unremarked upon. Retired for more than 35 years and widowed for more than 30, he lived alone in his flat – his eyesight and hearing failing but his mind pin-sharp – in self-imposed isolation. With friends and family gone or living abroad Henry, aged over 100 years, was facing an uncertain future alone, his past unnoticed and his place in history unheralded. Into this vacuum stepped Dennis Goodwin, co-founder of the World War One Veterans' Association, who persuaded a reluctant Henry to step outside his flat into the wider world. Dennis gradually formed a strong bond with the veteran, who at first didn't want to talk about the future or be reminded of the past. But with Dennis' gentle coaxing he was converted to a new way of thinking, that the men who laid down their lives in the First World War would slowly fade from public consciousness without Henry's timely intervention.

This friendship ultimately led Henry to talk freely about his fascinating past, once he realised it was a fitting way to pay tribute to all the millions who had fallen in the Great War. Along with other surviving veterans, Henry told his story in a BBC television documentary, as well as in various publications. Further, Dennis coaxed him into schools and other public arenas to tell his story, always highlighting the supreme sacrifice his generation had made. All the while, the number of veterans from the distant era dwindled. Today there are just three left who can recall the Great War at first hand.

Conversely, the relationship between these two men has grown and today it is almost like that of father and son. It is a connection based on trust, friendship, laughter and love. Through the past year Dennis has collated memories freely given by Henry that cover over a century of British history. It is a unique snapshot of our country's social history, told by a man who lived through it all.

This book, written with Dennis, is part of Henry's legacy, to mark the contribution not only of the glorious dead of the First World War but also those who survived. Equally it is a story of one man's dedication to pay tribute to men like Henry who gave so much. It has two voices as Henry gives us his recollections from the age of three, spanning the centuries from Edwardian England to modern Britain, while Dennis tells us historical facts he has culled over the years, often at Henry's request, which will help readers better understand the context of events. It has been a journey for both men that has been undertaken with humour and empathy, liberating joy and a few tears.

one

EARLY LIFE

THROUGH MORE THAN 11 decades I have banked many memories, the first of which is crawling up a flight of stairs to a landing. From the top of the stairs I could see a bearded man sitting up in bed. I had probably already heard him coughing. It was my father, Henry Thomas Allingham, who was suffering from tuberculosis. He died in September 1899 at the age of 29. Aged just three, I was soon scooped up and carried back downstairs, probably by my mother, Amy, fearful as tuberculosis was notoriously infectious. I remember that a wooden gate was soon installed so I couldn't do the same thing again.

After his death, when I was three years old, my mother and I went to live with her parents, Nanna and Grandpa Foster. The 1901 census shows I lived with my grandparents at 52 Verulam Avenue in Walthamstow, London, along with my mother and her brother Charles. While my mother went out to work I was cared for by Nanna.

It's there that my next memory of childhood comes to mind. For the first Christmas I spent in Walthamstow I was given a wooden yacht. Not too far away was reedy Clapton Pond, where the yacht was to make her maiden voyage.

At the time it was a good neighbourhood. Nearby Clapton had a strong Salvation Army presence; in 1890 William Booth bought the former asylum and re-named it Clapton Congress Hall. The family of Robert Baden-Powell, the founder of the Scouts Movement, lived in a house in Clapton.

I made friends with the sons of the local chemist. The Andrews lads lived a different life from me but made me most welcome. The family chauffeur let me sit in the car, one of the few around at the time. And their home had a greenhouse where a gardener raised delicate flowers such as orchids. It seemed like a different world to me. That early experience obviously had an effect as I have loved flowers all my life.

London has always been a notorious black spot for poverty, but the problem became worse in the wake of the Industrial Revolution, when hundreds of people arrived in the capital in search of jobs and homes. Victorian England had believed the poor to be shameful, assuming that drink and bad lifestyle choices had led to the predicament of many who thronged the narrow confines of city ghettos like those in London's East End. Although the rich lived close by, they turned their collective gaze away from the human tragedy unfolding in the next neighbourhood where residents suffered from hunger, were badly clothed, lived in squalor and were prone to diseases such as tuberculosis and cholera. When Henry was born, however, attitudes were on the cusp of change.

With the arrival of authors and social commentators who saw the downtrodden differently, society's awareness of the plight of the poor was heightened and a hitherto flinty approach began to soften. Charles Dickens (1812–1870) frequently and sympathetically portrayed the problems of poverty in his stories.

Spearheading a trend for philanthropy, Dr Thomas Barnardo had begun a chain of homes for destitute children by 1870. The National Society for the Prevention of Cruelty to Children (NSPCC) was in action in London in 1884, led by Rev. Benjamin Waugh. The first court case of child cruelty had already been prosecuted by the Royal Society for the Prevention of Cruelty to Animals.

Socialism was beginning to make an impact and in 1888 Annie Besant (1847–1933) helped engineer a strike at the Bryant & May matchstick company in Bow, east London, where workers were compelled to work with dangerous chemicals, were badly paid and were fined for trifling 'offences', including dropping matches. Emotions had already run high at the factory after all employees had a shilling deducted from their wages to pay for a statue of William Gladstone, a hero of factory owner Theodore Bryant. Meanwhile, Karl Marx was living in London in the vicinity of some of its poorest districts and these scenes of appalling deprivation may well have shaped his views that eventually evolved into communism.

In 1903 Charles Booth published his phenomenal Life and Labour of the People in London. *The book had taken 20 years to write, and in it Booth charted every street and its state of repair as well as its inhabitants. He translated the information onto a map and used black to mark the worst areas where the inhabitants were 'vicious semi-criminals'. By then Booth realised that severely deprived conditions had improved during those 20 years of writing – but that many desperate scenarios still existed. Some slums had been alleviated by new outer-city estates – but not all. The lack of sanitation, the root cause of many diseases, was being remedied. Yet still London's burgeoning poor population endured terrible hardships. An escape route, such as that offered by the Army, was often gleefully seized.*

Nanna and Grandpa Foster took me on holidays. During the summer of my fifth birthday we went to the Isle of Wight. One memory stands out from the trip. Grandpa was always interested in trains and carried timetables of the various train networks in his pocket. One day we arrived at a station, intending to catch the train to Shanklin, where we were staying in a seaside guesthouse. The station platform was deserted although, by Grandpa's timetable, we had just six minutes to wait. Six minutes came and went and no train arrived. Grandpa approached the door marked 'Stationmaster' and knocked. The first railway timetable was published in 1839 and by 1880 there were 40 different railway companies in existence in Britain with over 6,000 miles of track between them. Somehow the Shanklin train had left early despite the timetable.

An apologetic stationmaster consulted with Grandpa, who realised that another train was not due for an hour.

'Is it only you?' the stationmaster enquired.

'No, there is my wife and grandson,' said Grandpa.

'Well, there's a locomotive tender going to Shanklin in ten minutes. I am sure they will take you considering the situation.'

Grandpa seized the opportunity. I was rigid with excitement as I was lifted onto the tender and introduced to the driver and the firemen. Off the train puffed, with me clinging on to Grandpa and Nanna, who was terrified. The driver opened the throttle and, with a few bursts of the whistle, the train picked up speed. I can still recollect the violent swaying of the train and the clatter of the wheels on the track. It's a journey I have never forgotten.

When we drew up into the station yard at Shanklin, my Nanna produced her handkerchief and spat on it. She took a firm hold of me and vigorously tried to wipe off all the black soot that had showered my face and clothes during the journey. Not content with ruining one handkerchief, she claimed Grandpa's as well and the spit wash continued apace. Meanwhile, Grandpa invited the two railwaymen into a pub and treated them to a couple of pints of beer as thanks for their kindness.

Life in the Victorian age changed beyond compare after an explosion in technology that must have caused a sense of breathlessness at what could be achieved. A relatively short spell saw advances or inventions in the realms of communications, newspapers, transport, medicine and entertainment.

Although it seems quaint by today's standards, it was the invention of the telegraph that excited most people. Wire-borne signals had been developed independently in the USA and the UK but it was in 1866 that the nations were linked by the first successful transatlantic cable. It was only a matter of time before a global network was set in place. This in turn had a mighty impact on the speed at which newspapers could report world events. In the wake of the telegraph came the telegram, the telephone, a modern postal system and eventually the wireless radio, providing those in the late Victorian era with an efficient communications system that filled a previously silent void.

Inventors had been aware of electricity for years but only in the late nineteenth century was it harnessed for common usage. After 1880 it began appearing in households. Engineering ingenuity seemed to know no bounds. In 1896, the year Henry was born, the first large-scale hydro-electric plant was opened in Scotland and the first escalator appeared, in Coney Island, USA.

Coal was king and steam engines had been developed to increase the rate at which it could be extracted from mines. Steam engines also drove the textile industry, which clustered in areas where coal was plentiful. Factories were getting bigger and, slowly, becoming safer. In 1885 the clocking-on machine was developed, dictating the rhythm by which hundreds of thousands of British people would live their lives.

Public awareness about the dangers of bad sanitation were finally being raised. After the 'Great Stink' of 1858, an episode in which the smell from the polluted water of the Thames was so bad it made MPs in the nearby House of Commons gag, new laws governing the nation's sewage systems were wrought. Anaesthetics and antiseptics were introduced in hospitals and this was the era of Florence Nightingale (1820–1910), who did much to raise the profile of nursing care.

The following year Nanna and Grandpa decided on a holiday in Scarborough. What made the holiday so memorable was that we got to our destination by sea. We arrived at Millwall docks in London at about five in the afternoon to board SS *Claudius*, a freighter transporting scrap iron. The bit I remember most is that, shortly after we arrived in our cabin, there was a tremendous noise. I jumped out of my skin as tons of scrap iron were loaded into the hold. Still, the prospect of sleeping on board an actual ship at sea was thrilling.

It was foggy when we left the dock but after we cleared the River Thames, the weather lifted. While I was on board I met a black man for the first time. We were formally introduced and we shook hands. Afterwards, I remember examining my palm to see if any of the colour had rubbed off.

I spent most of the journey on deck with Grandpa, who pointed out many of the interesting features of the coastline. Little did I realise that, within a dozen years, I would be aboard a ship in the North Sea once more, this time heading for a rendezvous with the British home fleet before the momentous Battle of Jutland.

SS *Claudius* dropped anchor off Scarborough and we were taken ashore in a small boat. We stayed in a boarding house just off the sea front. Just like children today when they go to Scarborough, I spent most of the holiday playing on the sand but there was plenty to see and do, including a Punch and Judy show and many seaside vendors. One afternoon the Salvation Army band arrived and all the children, including me, gathered round. One Salvation Army fellow held a Bible aloft in one hand and bellowed: 'Come and be saved. We are all sinners. Follow us to the Citadel and be saved.'

Each sentence was punctuated with a bang on the big drum and cries of: 'Hallelujah! Come and be saved!' We got so caught up in the atmosphere that we did indeed follow them as they marched off towards the citadel. However, when we got there, not knowing what to expect next, the Salvationists – still holding aloft their bibles – glared at us all and we were then promptly all given our marching orders to 'clear off!' as it transpired they only wanted to save adults.

I was taken to Scarborough's music hall and felt really grown up. While we were there I'm certain we heard 'I'll Be Your Sweetheart' and 'Daisy Bell' ('A bicycle made for two'). The reason I can remember the last one is because I spent the rest of the holiday pestering Nanna for a bike.

Once, when I was really small, Nanna took me to Cromer in Norfolk. I had a bucket and spade and was delighted to play in the sand. Then I spotted all the children playing at the water's edge in the waves and I wanted to join them.

'Please let me go in the sea,' I implored.

'You can't go in because you haven't got any slips [trunks],' she said. But eventually she relented, on the condition that I put my hands over my 'teapot'. In those days bathing was quite a ceremony and you didn't see the larking around like the young people do today. Nanna gave me strict orders on how to behave and I was quite nervous making my way down to the water's edge, looking back at her for reassurance. I needn't have worried though for as soon as I was in I had a whale of a time.

I was having such an enjoyable time that I completely forgot I was naked and soon after I raced back up to her, waving my arms about and not giving any thought to my 'teapot' being on public display.

The next day, Nanna and I went for tea with friends. When the teapot appeared it was covered in a hand-knitted tea cosy.

Immediately, Nanna turned to me smiling and said, 'You could have done with one of those yesterday.'

This story continues over a hundred years later. In 2006, Nicki – the daughter of Dennis and Brenda Goodwin – was about to give birth and Henry had wanted to be kept informed as to her progress. Nicki successfully gave birth to a boy, Marcus, and the news was conveyed to Henry when Dennis visited him at his home the following day. A beaming Henry immediately announced 'It's got a teapot,' to everyone's hilarity.

By the time of Henry's childhood the British Empire encompassed four million square miles and a quarter of the world's population, bringing money, power and trade to Britain. Acquisition of the empire had begun in Tudor times and was largely represented by land in the Americas. As Britain lost control of America in the War of Independence in 1776, so it gained mastery of Australia.

But it was the spheres of interest sculpted by commercial enterprises during the nineteenth century that reaped perhaps the greatest rewards as the industrial age we know today took hold across the globe. India, of course, was the jewel in the crown. Queen Victoria was crowned Empress of India in 1876, although she never visited the country. Nonetheless, she cannot have failed to appreciate the wealth the subcontinent dispatched to Mother England.

Then there was the scramble for Africa, sparked by the barbarous rule of King Leopold of Belgium in the Congo. Hoping to tackle the excesses of Belgian rule – and not wishing to miss a trading opportunity – France, Germany and Britain clamoured for land on a continent that had never previously been divided by national boundaries.

The British prime minister Benjamin Disraeli (1804–1881) was a stalwart of imperialist foreign policy. It would, he believed, help to bring order to presumed chaos. It was a view coined by Rudyard Kipling (1865–1936) as 'the white man's burden', that is, the moral

*duty of Britain as the world's leader to police the globe, imposing its
own religious and economic principles along the way. Kipling was
among those who fondly imagined that Britain was an imperative
civilising influence. In fact, one of few enduring legacies of the Empire
was to have cars driving on the left-hand side of the road when much
of the rest of Europe and America plumped for the right.*

*William Gladstone (1809–1898), who succeeded Disraeli, was less
inclined towards imperialism. He could see that overseas forays might
become costly and so it proved when unrest in Egypt and Sudan put
the Suez Canal in peril. Independence movements flourished, notably
among the Boers in South Africa who tried to throw off the Empire's
shackles at the turn of the twentieth century. Britain claimed victory,
but fought without distinction. After the First World War, an empire
that had taken centuries to accrue unravelled in just a few decades.*

My mother used to take me to Hampstead Heath every Easter,
where there was always a huge fair. Thousands of people went and
I looked forward to this special treat. Just as today, fairgrounds were
a fascinating place for children, and grown ups for that matter, and
were extremely popular. It was a sea of colour and lights, which I
loved, as well as the noise and excitement.

Everywhere there were gaudily painted wagons and stalls. It was a
community on wheels. I rode the swing boats and carousels and slid
down the helter skelter. The ghost train was one of my favourites
and Mother always dragged me past the tunnel of love. I stood
for ages in front of the steam engines, absorbing the noise, smoke
and atmosphere. There were shooting galleries as well as coconut
shies. Gypsies in their heavily embellished costumes clinked their
way around the fairground, offering to tell fortunes. Boxing booths
enticed young men to come in and get a good hiding. There were
also dwarfs and bearded ladies and dancing bears. The noise of
barrel organ music vied with stall holders' shouts, urging people to

'roll up, roll up'. Countless attractions invited you to part with your hard-earned pennies.

On the way home, Mother always produced a chocolate bar without fail. It was the perfect end to a special day and I treasure those memories.

On 22 January 1901 Queen Victoria died at Osborne House on the Isle of Wight, aged 81. Since Prince Albert's death four decades earlier she had built up a custom of residing there at Christmas time. She died from a cerebral haemorrhage with her eldest son and heir Edward, as well as grandson Kaiser Wilhelm II of Germany, by her side. She had planned her own funeral, which took place on 2 February. Despite having spent 40 years of widowhood dressed in black, she insisted she would be buried in a white dress and her wedding veil and taken on a horse-drawn gun carriage to Windsor for burial. During the procession to Windsor, the horses broke loose from their harnesses. Royal Navy personnel then manhandled the carriage for the remainder of the journey. It truly was the end of an era as Queen Victoria embodied the soul of the country and indeed the British Empire – it had reached its zenith under her reign. The country and empire was plunged into mourning for weeks.

In August 1902 I remember being taken into the City of London to swell the numbers of people lining the streets for the coronation of King Edward VII. I sat on Grandpa's shoulders, waving a flag. I had only just learned to sing 'God Save the Queen'. Now there was a king and I had to change the words. Earlier, in May 1902, there had been great excitement as the Australian cricket team was bowled out for 36 runs at Edgbaston.

At the time of his coronation, Edward VII made his nephew, Kaiser Wilhelm II of Germany, a Field Marshal in the British Army. I hope the Kaiser did not receive the full salary!

A lord on his country estate and a labourer in the field are two stereotypes that perhaps ideally reflect the upper and lower classes that lived in Britain for centuries. Somewhere between the two were the 'middling sorts', including clerks and teachers. But when the population fell between two and six million, as it did in Britain for a long time, no social group was oversubscribed.

However, with increasing urbanisation came accelerating population growth. By 1851 the British population stood at 21 million and 50 years later the figure was 37 million. In the Victorian era, the middle classes mushroomed. Clear definitions about who fell into the boundaries of middle class were – and are – impossible. As the economy expanded there were a sizeable number of shop keepers, merchants and small-scale entrepreneurs who were far from the upper classes but could not rightly be described as working class either.

Of course, 'working class' implies unskilled labourers, such as those in factory jobs, working in mechanised transport and the relatively small number who remained in agriculture. There was still at this time many artisans. Then there was a burgeoning civil service. Some of the administrative jobs created were highly taxing while others were lowly clerical posts.

With a growing number of occupations, it was attitude of mind that many commentators applied to define class. The new middle classes tended towards perseverance, prudence and personal ambition. They thrived on being self-reliant and relished competition. Even those who made sufficient money to become substantial landowners did not resemble the long-established upper classes in attitude or behaviour.

The confines of class were very rigid and women, regarded as second-class citizens, felt this keenly. Working-class women tended to go out to work to help feed the family. Middle-class women were more likely to stay at home and look after children and household duties. However, neither were entitled to vote, and if they did work, their pay was much less than that of their male counterparts. The Suffragette movement, which fought for votes for women, didn't have universal backing either. Queen Victoria branded the notion of equal rights for women as 'mad, wicked folly'. But this didn't stop women led by Emmeline Pankhurst (1858– 1928) from pulling off numerous stunts to pressurise Parliament for change. Suffragettes carried out direct action such as chaining themselves to railings, setting fire to the contents of mailboxes, smashing windows and on occasions setting off bombs. One suffragette, Emily Davison, died after she stepped out in front of the King's horse, Anmer, at the Epsom Derby of 1913. Many of her fellow suffragettes were imprisoned and went on hunger strikes, during which they were restrained and forcibly fed. The infamous Cat and Mouse Act was passed by the British government to prevent suffragettes from obtaining public sympathy; it provided the release of those whose hunger strikes had brought them sickness, as well as their re-imprisonment once they had recovered.

Attitudes towards women and class changed following the outbreak of war when due to wholesale conscription there was a severe shortage of manpower. Women then worked in all trades on the home front showing they could successfully fill the void and keep the country's economy and war effort going. After a government rallying call made in 1915, women delivered coal, drove taxis and made armaments. Yet it wasn't until 1918 that women aged over 30 with a property qualification were finally given the lawful right to vote. Parity was finally established in the year of Pankhurst's death.

What else can I remember about life when I was a boy? Motorcars had not yet arrived so all transport was horse-drawn, even buses. There were individual tradesmen's carts delivering bread, milk, groceries and coal. Milk was carried in steel churns holding up to 15 gallons and dispensed to customers who brought their own containers to carry it home. Today's health and safety officials would have had a field day, but that was how it was in those days.

Shops had counters and shelves holding jars of tea, cocoa, biscuits and so forth. Sugar, rice and dried fruits were stored in hessian sacks and weighed out on demand. Carcasses hung from hooks at the butchers, where there was often a pig's head staring out at you. Coal was the most essential fuel, used in fires, for shipping, for railways and in industry. Street lighting was provided by gas, with a small army of lamplighters responsible for igniting the mantle. The dim lights cast eerie shadows on the pavements. On the streets you could often find entertainers eking out a living, especially barrel organ-grinders ringing out the hits of the day.

The postal service was probably better than today's. A postcard cost one halfpenny, letters one penny. In the City of London and a few places elsewhere there were same-day deliveries.

The main thing one can say of how much better off we are today is that life expectancy in that era was much less than it is now. Tuberculosis, diphtheria and fevers were common and often fatal – as was the case with the early death of my father. Cancer never appeared on death certificates as it couldn't be easily detected as it can be now – but it still existed. Our sense of community was very strong, and most people died at home and were laid out by neighbours and friends. Funerals were more commonplace and almost always started from home – it was the natural thing to do. In those days there was a great deal of nostalgia and reverence over death. Those in mourning wore black for 12 months, then a black ribbon around their arm for even longer. Queen Victoria was still wearing black when I was born, and her husband died in 1861.

There were pubs on just about every street corner. Men saw them as an escape from hard work or more often than not their womenfolk. There used to be a lot of fights and rowdy behaviour – that was a common sight back then and the police were more on hand to sort it out. Women were not barred from pubs but they were out of sight in the snug, leaving the men to their business.

two

LIFE IN EDWARDIAN ENGLAND

I WENT TO GAMUEL Road School in Walthamstow at the age of five in 1901. I don't know what I was expecting but this wasn't it. Out of the 40 or more children in my class, the majority were poorly dressed, had no shoes and quickly resorted to fights.

Boys wore short trousers until their legs got hairy. Girls wore combinations (all-in-one vests and pants) – I know that because I saw them on washing lines. Shoes were always a problem, at least well-fitting shoes were. I have had two hammer toes all my life thanks to badly fitting shoes.

At school we were taught how to read and write and how to add up. As Nanna had given me lessons at home, I was way out in front of everyone else. We had sandboxes to write in. I'll always remember the smell given off by the sand. It ponged. We had to trace the letters in sand using a metal skewer. And there was trouble if anyone spilt the sand. Later we were given slates and chalk. To clean the slate you had to use saliva on a cloth that was passed among us. Slate pencils were also used sometimes but they made a horrible screeching sound. Any books we had were shared and dog-eared.

While I was there I met a boy who liked to throw his weight around. He was taller than most of us in the class and soon reduced quite a number to tears. I soon fell foul of him and got a good hiding. There was nothing I could do to stop him throwing punches. When I arrived home the worse for wear, Nanna patched me up as best she could. Charlie, Mother's younger brother, called in that night. When he heard about what had happened he decided to help.

Every evening for three weeks he taught me how to box. Charlie, a wooden box maker, told me to keep out of this bully's way until he decided I was ready to defend myself. And he told me to take advantage by throwing the first punch, following it immediately with a second. Always stand up to bullies, he told me. And he said that if I was knocked down, I was to get up straight away.

Finally he decided I was ready to look after myself. Soon afterwards, I felt a shove in the back and turned around to see this lad. Immediately I went towards him with my fists raised. I landed the first blow in his stomach followed by a left jab that got his face and nose. As he cried out and covered his face, I got one more punch in. Then it was all over. The lad ran off, beaten. I couldn't wait to go home that night and tell Uncle Charlie what had happened.

The boxes made by Charlie were sturdier than those of today. They were used to transport soap from the wholesalers to the shops. Some were made to carry household items. It was these that were used by orators in London who wanted to deliver political messages to the public, hence the phrase 'get off your soap box'. As a young man I loved hearing people on soap boxes. I think that personal touch is missing from politics today.

Until the late nineteenth century there was a haphazard approach to education in England. The churches had run schools since the Middle Ages that centred on reading the scriptures, but there was no uniformity about provision. There were also ragged schools which were run, as the name implies, for poor children, usually with philanthropists picking up the bills. Only a few voices called for a wider and deeper spread of education. And there was a surprising amount of opposition to any notion of 'education for all'.

The rich had access to private, fee-paying schools for their own children. However, many wealthy people saw no need to educate the poor. It would only ferment discontent among agricultural workers, servants and factory employees, they reasoned. Radical movements in Europe like the French Revolution at the end of the eighteenth century had proved just how volatile people outside the aristocracy could be.

Meanwhile many poor families had no reason to seek education for their children. It cost money that was hard to come by. And if there were many mouths in the family to feed, then the children needed to work to help pay for food or otherwise they would be sent to the workhouse. East London was alive with sweatshops that welcomed child labour. Although the employment of children aged nine or under was forbidden in 1933, there was little enforcement of the law. Indeed, factory acts had just as much influence on the development of schools as education law. Only when child labour issues were tackled could schools finally expect to flourish.

In 1870 the School Act saw the country divided into districts, each with an education board. The board ran fee-paying schools with a restricted curriculum alongside those provided by the churches, organising charitable donations for the poorest children. Now teachers tended to be paid more working for the board schools than ever they did at rival church schools. The act also signalled the arrival of the board men or attendance officers, much-feared figures who visited the homes of absentees. While they generally looked sympathetically upon a girl staying home to do chores and look after younger siblings, they would be altogether harder on boys who had been tempted to miss school for work.

Ten years later school became compulsory for children aged between five and ten. In 1891 Parliament made education effectively free when a long-running battle by the country's aristocracy opposed to government intervention with taxpayers' money in the arena of education was finally lost. By 1899 the school leaving age was set at 12 and, less than 20 years later, it was raised to 14. All the while, the range of subjects studied at school was broadening and even began to include sports and science.

However, conditions at school were often far from benign. Use of the cane and other physical abuses were commonplace. Boys might expect to be picked up by the ears or cuffed around the head for minor misdemeanours. Only sustained campaigning among a relatively small number of people eventually succeeded in scaling down corporal punishment until its abolition in 1987.

I left Gamuel Road School at Easter 1902 and went to Bessborough Road School. In June I remember watching soldiers home from the Boer War parading in front of the Town Hall in Hackney – troops known as the Clapton volunteers.

After I returned to school following the summer holidays, I broke my leg. I was playing leapfrog over the backs of classmates and I was in mid-air when a girl ran across where I planned to land. I tried to avoid her by swerving in mid-air, only to collapse in a heap and injure my leg. It was a clean break and I had great fun showing off the plastered leg.

I didn't like school and that's because I didn't learn enough. I always felt as though I was waiting for the rest of the class to catch up. And it was learning by rote, which wasn't very inspiring even for people like me who wanted to learn. Discipline was strict, too. There was always the threat of the cane.

When I was seven, Nanna arranged for me to have piano lessons. My teacher, Professor Tom McGuire, also kept a pet shop. I often tried to get to the shop early so that I could look at the snakes and other animals and birds. I used the tram to travel from home to the professor's house. Often, when the trams were full, the conductor failed to get around to me and other passengers and that's when I found myself a penny better off. I practised hard and always kept up with the exercises the professor had set me.

Even at the very early stages of my tuition I was constantly pestered by Nanna to play a piece. I knew I wasn't ready for any kind of public performance so I kept putting her off. Eventually Nanna had her day when I came home with my first prepared piece, 'The Bluebells of Scotland'. I got a big kiss and a cuddle from a proud grandparent.

In 1903 I went to the Oval to see W.G. Grace play. He walked like an elderly person because his pads were too long for him. Records at the Oval show W.G. Grace played there on 9, 10 and 11 July and made 15 in the first innings and 19 in the second innings.

Henry witnessed W.G. Grace (1848–1915) at the crease in the twilight of his illustrious career. Born into a family of cricketing fanatics, William Gilbert Grace, also known as WG, Gilly, Gilby or Willy, was a record-breaking cricketer. In 1895 he notched up his 100th century and, in May of that year alone, scored more than 1,000 runs. In 1871 he scored a double century in two matches. His batting average overall was just under 40 per innings, at a time when pitches were rough and batting totals much lower than they are today. But that includes the scores of later matches, when he was aged over 50 and turning in less ebullient performances. He was also renowned for his bowling and, memorably, got all the wickets in one match he played. But batting was his first love. He once advised other captains: 'Take what the gods have offered. When you win the toss, always bat. If the conditions suit bowling, think about it. Then always bat.'

He is also remembered as the first England captain who surrendered the Ashes to Australia at the end of the 1891–2 tour. Grace also trained as a doctor and had a practice in one of the poorest areas of Bristol, frequently treating patients without charge. His final game was in 1914, a year before he died from a stroke.

At the beginning of 1904 I went to Fourth Avenue School in Manor Park. The headmaster was Mr Sam Whittaker and there was a teacher called Mr Varsey, a bluecoat boy having been educated at one of the schools traditionally established to educate the poor. Mr Varsey was an officer in the Territorial Army and trained men in the use of machine guns. After he returned from army camps held during school holidays, he would tell us all about the experience.

It was at this school that I discovered sport. I loved playing football and cricket. Football was coached after school at a cost of a halfpenny a session. Some of the Fourth Avenue players went on to play for West Ham. I made the first team and was proud of my footballing skills.

Mr Whittaker was also a referee in charge of some of the first division games. He told us all about local clubs: how Millwall was a works team from a jam factory, that West Ham used to be known as 'Thames Ironworks' and that Tottenham was once part of a cricket club. One day he called me into his study. I owed five and a half pennies for the football training sessions. He was prepared to waive the payments but I wouldn't hear of it. I would find the money from somewhere.

When I suggested doing a paper round to earn some money for myself, Mother's reply was short, sharp and negative. So I built myself a box cart of wood mounted on a set of wheels I found abandoned in a field. I liberated a shovel from the outhouse and went out into the streets where I knew there would be a plentiful supply of horse dung. To me, horses were animals that were dangerous at both ends and uncomfortable in the middle. But at least they were creatures of habit and I knew just where to find the mounds of muck that I would change into brass.

When I had loaded the cart, I went from door to door offering manure for sale at a price of three pennies per load. It was very popular as people either composted it or added water to make it into liquid fertiliser, ideal for growing tomatoes, which plenty of people did. Some folk probably paid up to get away from the sound of those squeaking wheels. After I'd paid my debts I had spare money for a boy's magazine or a chocolate bar.

One day I was on my way to deliver a full load when I was stopped by a man standing outside his house who demanded: 'What have you got there?'

If you can't see it, surely you can smell it, I thought to myself. But I didn't want to be rude so I told him it was manure.

'How much are you charging for it?'

'Threepence,' I told him.

'It's a bit ripe, I'll give you tuppence,' said the man.

I stood my ground and demanded threepence but he told me again it was only worth tuppence. At that I walked off with my trolley, ready to look for more-obliging customers. As I was heading off, over the clatter of the wheels on the road I heard him cry out that he would pay threepence after all. I didn't look around, though, or break my stride. I knew I would have no problem selling it elsewhere. Always trust your judgement – that's a lesson I learned early in life.

Of course, I made some money out of this enterprise but it was short-lived. I had to hide the wagon from my mother for a start. She had no idea what I was up to. Then I had a transport problem when somebody stole it. There was no point getting too upset. Cars and lorries were rapidly replacing horse-drawn vehicles. I knew that the supply was drying up and the bottom dropped out of the market.

Aged nine, I left my grandparents' home and went to live with Mother again in London. There were no more holidays after that until the weekend that war broke out.

'To be born an Englishman is to win first prize in the lottery of life.' So said Cecil Rhodes, the man who founded Rhodesia on behalf of the British Empire. His words reflect the prestige attached to Britain at the time, unchallenged as ruler of the waves and known as the workshop of the world. Britain's pre-eminence in the global order could not be disputed.

But Britain was going to need more than mere jingoism to keep its place at the top of the pile. Only the fossilised minds of the few believed it was a God-given right for Britain to lead and for the rest of the world to follow. Others were looking nervously over their shoulders as the nineteenth century drew to a close, at other European nations poised to purloin some of the planet's riches for themselves.

Germany was one obvious candidate as chief rival. The country was unified by Chancellor Otto von Bismarck (1815–1898) after a series of conflicts in the middle of the nineteenth century. Within its borders there were Polish, Danish and French minorities. But Kaiser Wilhelm II had even greater imperialist ambitions and looked towards both Africa and the Pacific to enhance the newly emerging German empire.

If Britain wasn't eyeing Germany with suspicion, neighbouring France certainly was. In 1871 France had been defeated by Prussia, which formed the core of the new Germany. Still railing at the unfairness of it all and keen to bolster its prestige, France was certainly not intending to be outdone in terms of imperialism, especially in Africa.

For its part, Britain still held France with some suspicion as the victory over Napoleon at Waterloo in 1815 seemed a comparatively fresh memory. However, British concern centred mostly on Russia, whose activities in Asia and Eastern Europe were making politicians decidedly uncomfortable. That led to Afghanistan becoming a buffer between Russia and India, at enormous cost to both its people and British soldiers.

Meanwhile America was licking its wounds after the damaging civil war of the 1860s. Taxes were high there but confidence was growing. With the Spanish-American War of 1898 the US claimed some outposts of its own, including Cuba and the Philippines.

Thus every nation had its own compelling reasons to be both fearful and moderately aggressive. Africa was something of a blank canvas and it was there that the global colonisers went to work.

THE BOER WAR

The Second Boer War – commonly referred to as the Boer War – was fought from 11 October 1899 until 31 May 1902, between the British Empire and the two independent Boer republics of the Orange Free State and the South African Republic (Transvaal Republic).

The origins of the war were complex, resulting from over two centuries of conflict between the Boers and the British over a variety of policies such as land, gold deposits and emigration into the main Boer territory of the Transvaal and the Orange Free State. Britain, spoiling for a war, met its match in the tenacity of the Boers, shown over the three years of conflict, led magnificently by their president Paul Kruger. It was a brutal campaign notable for atrocities on both sides, a scorched-earth policy that destroyed thousands of Boer homesteads, two major defeats for the British Army, and the introduction of the concentration camp – which led to the deaths of thousands of Boer civilians suffering from malnutrition and disease.

An eventual settlement of hostilities was finally reached with the Treaty of Vereeniging in 1902. The two Republics were absorbed into the British Empire, although the British were forced to make a number of concessions and reparations to the Boers. The granting of limited autonomy for the area ultimately led to the establishment of the Union of South Africa. The war had a lasting effect on the region and on British domestic politics. The war, known as the last British imperial war, came at a cost of over £200 million to the taxpayer, and was viewed as the most disastrous the Empire had fought, until the Great War in 1914. Britain's potential adversaries cast eager eyes over how the British Army had inadequately performed against what was a well-motivated militia – it did not boost Britain's image, rather it increased the desire of Germany to take her on and build an empire for the impatient Kaiser.

Usually I played in the streets after school was over with friends who were always keen for a game. When we played football we used coats for goalposts. But I preferred cricket, had my own bat and used the lampposts for wickets. Uncle Charlie did a lot of skipping to keep himself fit and I made my own skipping rope, which I still have in the garage of my Eastbourne home. Sometimes I skipped with the girls.

I became friendly with a boy called Smithy who had a sister. All three of us went out and played together. At the time I often used to ask my mother, 'Why can't I have a sister, just like Smithy?' Smithy's father was a butcher who often brought beef puddings home. I relished the meals I had in the Smith household.

In 1904 work began on a new public library, which still stands today. The Carnegie Library in Romford Road, Manor Park, was built with money donated by philanthropist Andrew Carnegie (1835–1919); it was one of several he added to London's East End. The library included elaborate terracotta features, including a bust of Carnegie. I joined the library as soon as it opened in 1905 and was issued with ticket 13. That meant I could take one book out at a time.

Life changed for me when I contracted measles at the age of ten, during the school summer holidays. To recover I was sent to Kent to stay with Mr and Mrs Kitchen, friends of the family who had no children of their own. They ran a smallholding close to the main London to Dover railway line.

I can remember going to the railway cutting to watch the express train thundering through at 60 mph. It was a spectacular sight, with smoke pouring from its funnel and the glow of flames in the engine. I found machinery and its capabilities fascinating. But I also loved life on the farm. I looked after the pigs and learned to milk a cow. One day I was late for milking and the shed seemed to be deserted. I called out for Mr Kitchen but there was no reply. Eventually I peered over the stable-style door to be greeted with a stream of milk in the face. Mr Kitchen had taken aim after hiding behind a cow. He jumped up, roaring with laughter. I loved my time there so much that I thought one day I would also be a farmer.

In the summer of 1907 my mother and I moved to South Lambeth Road in Clapham. My mother asked if I could be a pupil at the London County Council High School, sited in the same road. Headmaster Frederick Rabey told her it was too late, the entrance exams had been completed and the new term had started. Still, she persuaded him to give me a shot at it.

I felt gnawing anxiety as I was led from the headmaster's study to a huge hall to sit an exam. But Mr Rabey's fatherly manner helped to ease the tension. 'Remember, make haste slowly,' he told me as he produced the paper. I managed to answer all the questions – some better than others. Anyway, I did enough to get a place as a pupil. I was filled with excitement at the prospect of learning new subjects like art, science, French and metalwork.

Soon I bought a correspondence course as well, and went to evening classes at the Regent Street Polytechnic, which is where fliers in the Royal Flying Corps were later taught. [Formerly the Young Men's Christian Institute, the Regent Street Polytechnic was established in 1891 and lasted for 80 years until combining with another London college to become the London Polytechnic. In 1992 the polytechnic became the University of Westminster.] In the end I juggled all three to fill my appetite for education.

In October 1907 the whole school was led outside to see the first British airship on its flight from Aldershot to London. It circled around St Paul's Cathedral, although plans to return to Hampshire were halted by strong winds and the 120-ft *Nulli Secundus* put down at Crystal Palace.

Our sports lessons were inspired in 1908 by the arrival of the Olympic Games in London. My schoolmates and I ran and re-ran races. Football was becoming increasingly popular after the English team played its first international against Austria, winning by six goals to one. Also, I had learned to swim and mimicked the Australian crawl. [Developed at the turn of the twentieth century by Richard Cavill in Sydney, Australia, the stroke became known as front crawl after 1950.]

Every morning the school day began with hymns and the Lord's Prayer in the main hall. My favourite hymn was 'Holy, Holy, Holy', one that I'd like sung at my funeral. I could never have guessed that 96 years later I would be reciting the Lord's Prayer again, this time at the Cenotaph in Whitehall in front of a huge crowd, with television cameras recording it for an audience of more than a million.

I also went to the Salvation Army services held for children on Sunday afternoons. They were popular with boys and girls, probably because their parents wanted them out of the way. Still, I enjoyed the Bible stories .The teacher was a Salvation Army 'soldier' who was seeing the Superintendent's daughter Ada on the quiet. That sort of thing was frowned on at the time. However, Ada's brother George was in my class and knew all about it.

Usually, the teacher implored us to ask questions at the end of the class which was always met by averted eyes and shuffling feet. Well, this particular Sunday, George – one of the lads in my class – button-holed me as he wanted me to wanted me to ask a question at the end of the lesson. I didn't want to do it and said 'Go and ask him yourself.' George said he couldn't as it was about his Ada. I crossly said it wasn't the right sort of question for a bible class and we walked in and sat down together at our desks.

At the end of the lesson, the teacher again asked if we had any questions, but I remained silent. George hissed at me "Ask him about Ada Henry," and the boys behind me started joining in, making me feel flustered. Noticing the commotion, the teacher looked in our direction and said, "Boys, have you something to ask me?'

'Henry has a question sir,' George announced to my consternation, and he pushed me making me knock my bible to the floor.

The teacher by now was walking down from his platform at the front of the class and towards where we were sitting, beaming, happy someone wanted to ask a question. What could I say?

I blurted out, 'Please, Sir, what were you doing in the park last night with Ada?'

Immediately, the teacher jumped up from his seat, grabbed me by the scruff of the neck and frogmarched me to the door.

'You wicked boy. Don't ever come back here. You are expelled,' he roared.

I felt thoroughly miserable – I knew I couldn't tell my mother what had happened without getting into even more trouble. So every Sunday I went to the Tate Gallery instead of the Salvation Army. Later the Salvation Army teacher came to see my mother to apologise. That was the first she had heard of the incident. Really though, that George did me a good turn because I loved those visits, especially seeing the Constables and other great works of art. My love for Constable's paintings allowed me later in life when I was married to actually take Dorothy to view the real-life scenes he has captured, when we holidayed with the girls in Norfolk.

In 1865 a new evangelical church movement was launched by William Booth. Its target was not the wealthy or the middle classes, which were generally the mark of existing churches. His mission was specifically to touch the lives of the poor, hungry and homeless.

Not only did he want to help the poor, he wanted to encourage them to help others. He went into pubs and backstreets, into slums and tenements, to spread the Christian message. By a happy accident, he discovered that accompaniment by a brass band drowned out the cat calls from sceptical observers and generally helped counter any hostile reception.

By any standards, Booth's initiative was laudable. But it is especially so given the prevailing negative attitude towards the poor, which is perhaps best illustrated by the Poor Law Amendment Act of 1834 that seemed designed to punish rather than to help as they brought in the infamous workhouses.

Workhouses were designed to look like prisons and functioned along similar lines. The diet was paltry. In 1845 a scandal erupted when it was discovered that workhouse inmates were so hungry they stripped decaying meat from the bones they had been crushing. All workhouse jobs were both arduous and tedious, and might have included corn milling, sack making, spinning or stone crushing.

The belief was that the threat of the workhouse would coax the poor to industry and even save on the spiralling cost of poor relief. Of course, few who found themselves within its walls had sufficient control over

*their lives to escape its clutches. Typically, orphans, the injured and
the mentally ill would find themselves with no other option. By 1926
there were some 226,000 people inside 600 workhouses nationwide.
In 1929 the Local Government Act officially abolished workhouses
although in practice they existed until long after this date.*

I spent a lot of the holidays with my cousin Sid Wheeler who
had joined the Scout Movement. When he told me what he
got up to in the Scouts I was desperate to join. But my mother
made it clear we could not afford the uniform or the expense of
Scouting events. One day Sid arrived in his uniform and badges
and insisted I accompanied him to a Scouting event in Victoria
Park. Although I didn't have a uniform, Sid told all the senior
Scouts at the gate that I was in his group and that my uniform
had not arrived in time. He even paid for me to go in. The senior
Scout on the gate nodded me through.

The activities held throughout the day were great fun but the
best part was the evening when we sat around the campfire, singing
songs. There was a huge sense of camaraderie. But despite my
enthusiasm I never joined the Scouts, for want of spare money.
Sid joined the Army in 1915 and served in France. In 1919 he
emigrated to Canada as part of a settlement scheme and bought his
own farm. I kept in touch with Sid through his sister Madeleine.

*Robert Stephenson Smyth Baden-Powell (1857–1941) was a major
general at the age of 43 during the defence of Mafeking in 1899, at the
start of the Second Boer War. It was here, during a 217-day siege, that he
observed how young people responded well to being given responsibility
for jobs and wrote his first book called* Aids to Scouting.

*When he returned to England in 1903 he found that his book
was being used by teachers and youth leaders across the country. In
1907 he held an experimental camp on Brownsea Island in Poole,*

Dorset, bringing together 22 boys from various backgrounds in what was a ground-breaking event. Scouting for Boys *was published the following year and the Scout Movement spread across the British Commonwealth, and soon all over the world.*

On the outbreak of the Great War, Baden-Powell put himself at the disposal of the War Office. No command, however, was given him, Lord Kitchener himself commenting that 'he could lay his hand on several competent divisional generals but could find no one who could carry on the invaluable work of the Boy Scouts'. Baden-Powell was reputedly believed to be then engaged in spying, and intelligence officers took great care not to dispute this myth.

By the time I was 13 I was doing really well at school and my mother was proud of my school reports. I found a talent in woodwork and metalwork and I always took my handiwork home to be closely inspected by my mother, Uncle Charlie and Auntie Rosie.

There was a political crisis in 1909 when Chancellor Lloyd George (1863–1945) had his 'people's budget' thrown out by the House of Lords. It was, he insisted, a war budget:

> It is for raising money to wage implacable warfare against poverty and squalidness. I cannot help hoping and believing that before this generation has passed away, we shall have advanced a great step towards that good time, when poverty, and the wretchedness and human degradation which always follows in its camp, will be as remote to the people of this country as the wolves which once infested its forests.

Eventually the budget was passed but I can't say it worked. I am part of that generation and there is still poverty today.

In 1910 King Edward VII died. I can remember the funeral cortège winding its way from Westminster Abbey, where the king had lain in state, to Paddington Station, from where his body was taken to St George's Chapel, Windsor, for burial. Thousands of people lined the streets that day.

The following year I was at the edge of more headlines. In January 1911 I was visiting Uncle Charlie and Auntie Rosie when there was a knock at the door. A tall man with a bandaged hand entered.

'I'll get you some tea. And a drop of the hard stuff,' said Rosie immediately.

'By the look of it, he needs it,' laughed Charlie. 'How's the hand?'

'Improving,' said the stranger.

'Tell Henry what's gone on,' said Charlie.

I found out that the stranger was Detective Constable Tom Dyer, a plain-clothes policeman with London's Metropolitan force. Three weeks before he had been one of a number of police officers to interrupt a robbery at a jewellery shop in Houndsditch, east London. Three policemen were killed and Tom was injured as several men made their getaway.

The men were anarchists, the police discovered, trying to fund a revolution in Russia. Within weeks it was known that the two gang leaders were in Sidney Street in east London. The place was surrounded and Home Secretary Winston Churchill arrived on the scene, as did a platoon of Scots Guards. At least the terrorists stood and fought, not like the indiscriminate suicide bombers that we know today.

After DC Dyer left that day, Charlie told me another story about him. On his way back to the police station Dyer spotted a man standing on the pavement near Hatton Garden reading a newspaper. The newspaper, Dyer noticed, was upside down. Dyer – suspecting the man was a lookout – rushed back to the station and alerted officers, who arrived just in time to catch three men running from a jewellery shop clutching their loot. Dyer received a commendation and a promotion for his initiative.

The gun battle that erupted in London in January 1911 was the culmination of anarchist activity in the capital over three years. First indications of a criminal cell from overseas at work in London came to light two years earlier when two armed Russian Latvians stole a factory payroll. Three died in the ensuing chase – a policeman, a robber and a ten-year-old bystander.

Many Latvians had come to London as refugees following a crackdown in their own country after a failed revolt in 1905. For many, the aim was to accrue enough cash and resources to return to Russia – which governed Latvia – and engineer a successful revolution that would remove the Tsarist regime.

Perhaps to that end, a group of Latvians raided a jewellery shop in Houndsditch in December 1910. Three unarmed policemen were killed alongside one of the would-be robbers. It was tip-off information about this gang that led to several arrests and finally brought the police to 100 Sidney Street three weeks later. But any hopes that the remaining gang members would come quietly were soon dashed when approaching police were sprayed with pistol fire.

Armed police were already posted at the scene but discovered that their small arms were no match for the high-calibre weapons wielded by the Latvians. Home Secretary Winston Churchill soon arrived at the scene, along with reinforcements from the Scots Guards, based at the Tower of London. Plans to storm the building or use field artillery against it were put on hold when wisps of smoke were seen coming from a window and soon developed into a blaze.

Churchill stopped the fire brigade from entering the building, fearing the men of the service would be in peril. Soon it became apparent that the fire had taken hold and all guns outside were pointed towards the front door, where the men were likely to emerge. None appeared.

Finally the ceiling and upper floors collapsed and all sounds of gunfire ceased. Firemen were trying to prevent damage to other buildings when a wall collapsed, burying five people, one of whom died in hospital. Two charred bodies were ultimately recovered from the wreckage. A third man, Peter Piaktow or 'Peter the Painter', had vanished. There has been speculation since that this man, thought to be the leader of the group, didn't even exist. Prosecutions of those believed to be linked to the gang later failed. One man in the dock was Jacob Peters, who returned to Russia after being freed and later became the deputy head of the Bolshevik secret police. He is thought to have died in Stalin's purges of the 1930s.

As for Churchill, he was barracked in Parliament for attending the scene, by his own admission more out of curiosity than necessity. However, he kept one memento from the day – the top hat that he wore complete with bullet hole.

three

FIRST JOB

AT THE AGE OF 15 I left school. My father had worked in the family firm, which was ironmongery, but it wasn't for me. His brother, Uncle Dick, was a director of an ironmongery company but I never had much to do with him. His other brother, Uncle Will, was the chef at the Bank of England. When I went to see him there he'd give me steak and eggs for breakfast.

My father's father, George Frederick Allingham, was a jewel-case designer and maker. A jolly man, he always used to wear a red Turkish fez with a black tassel and played games with me. He owned a factory that employed about 18 people. The cases produced there were usually for pieces of jewellery or silver cutlery. There was a lot of demand for presentation cases back then and I've still got a ring case that he made at the factory. It's a lovely piece of work.

Anyway, a firm of surgical instrument makers called Arnolds approached the school, looking for a trainee and offering a weekly wage of 12 shillings and sixpence, or 63 pence in today's money. I was recommended for the job thanks to my skills in metalwork and woodwork.

I rushed to tell my mother. At the time she was working at Tilbury Steam Laundry as a supervisor, in charge of a workforce some 180 strong. The company handled all the laundry from the ships docking at Tilbury, on the Thames estuary, and she lodged in the area. I told her it would not be long before I was earning enough money for her to give up work.

One day a week I went to St Bart's Hospital in the City of London to get experience in the use, care and maintenance of surgical instruments. Lunch was always meat pud and potato. While I was there, though, I was expected to clean and disinfect hospital equipment. I was doing jobs that no one else wanted to do. That's just one of the reasons I found life as a trainee mundane.

Within three months I had joined Carters, a company I passed going to and from work that worked on Foden three-ton wagons and lorries. The wage was 21 shillings, or £1.10, a week. It was manual labour and there was little opportunity to show flair.

I carried on with evening classes, where I became friendly with a lad who was working for Gordon's of East Dulwich, a car- and coach-builder. He tipped me off that Gordon's was looking to increase its labour force so I handed in my notice again to join the car manufacturing business. The quality of work expected at Gordon's was much higher than at Carter's. During the first week I didn't work at my best. The second week, though, I put in lots more effort and was given permanent employment.

My wage packet went up to 29 shillings, or £1.45 in today's money. I was delighted with that, especially after Uncle Charlie told me it was almost as much as the bowler-hatted gents in the City earned. In 1911, after the National Insurance Act was passed, I had to pay four pennies a week into the new scheme, with Gordon's paying three pennies and the government two pennies. The money went towards sickness and unemployment benefits.

I had to leave home soon after 5 a.m. each morning so I could start work at 6 a.m. There were two meal breaks, the first between 8 a.m. and 8.30 a.m. for breakfast and the second between noon and 12.30 p.m. for lunch. Usually I took in my own food. I took an egg and a slice of bacon for breakfast. There was always a fire in the smithy so I found a pan and went in there to cook. Some of the older men used a shovel rather than a pan. I had an enamel cup for tea and made a brew from water heated on the smithy fire.

Nanna made up my lunch, which I carried in my toolbox. But sometimes, for a treat, I would buy myself a piece of steak and cook it at work. You could get a really chunky piece of steak for between ten pennies and a shilling (five pence in today's money). I got the pan white-hot before cooking the meat and it was always delicious. Younger boys working at Gordon's took orders for food from the local shops. That could include anything from pies to sandwiches and cans of soup. You kept food in your toolbox because if there were any vermin around, they couldn't get at it there. I had been at work a year when the *Titanic* sank, claiming more than 1,500 lives.

The nineteenth century ushered in the age of the train. After George Stevenson's famous Rocket steam engine appeared in 1825, there was a feverish spell of line building until the rail network spread its tentacles to every town of note in Britain. By 1845 there were 2,441 miles of track that carried 30 million passengers each year. And expansion continued rapidly. Journeys that had once taken days by uncertain highway and horse and cart now took only hours as steam locomotives grew rapidly in capacity.

But it wasn't an entirely straightforward process. Track-builders across the country used no fewer than five different widths, which meant that engines and rolling stock that could operate on one line could not transfer to the next. And the boom in train freight spelled disaster for the canal system, which swiftly fell into disuse. Today, the train-builders' legacy includes the embankments and viaducts, the tunnels and bridges, and some iconic station buildings, all of which remain despite cuts in services.

Trains then evolved so they could run underground – a huge bonus in cities like London where streets were cramped with horses, carts and pedestrians. The first and most primitive underground line in London ran between Paddington and Farringdon and was opened in 1863. Steam from the train engines poured upwards through its tunnel's largely open roof. By 1890 the trains running underground were powered by electricity, as were trams running on the roads above.

By the end of the nineteenth century, push bikes had become better designed, more accessible and marginally more comfortable. But the greatest innovation in travel was the motorcar. Hidebound by the Red Flag Act of 1865, which demanded that cars travelled no faster than walking pace and were preceded by someone waving a flag, there at first seemed little future for troublesome, noisy cars. But vehicle technology improved quickly and the laws governing speed were ultimately relaxed.

Ships were also enjoying something of a heyday. Improved communications meant that the world was shrinking and there was more demand for transatlantic crossings than ever before. The mighty four-funnelled RMS Titanic was built in response to this and was tipped to cross the Atlantic faster than any other vessel. Its publicity material boasted that the Titanic was 'designed to be unsinkable'.

In the event, the ship, travelling at speed, hit an iceberg on 14 April 1912 and its supposedly water-tight compartments were breached. The drama of the night's events is familiar, with people scrambling for lifeboats before the ship tipped upright and slid down into the water. One survivor, wireless operator Harold Bride, who swam for his life from the stricken ship to a lifeboat, later recalled how the band was still playing as the Titanic was swallowed by the Atlantic. Although upwards of 700 people survived, the death toll stood at more than

1,500. On board were some of the most influential figures of the era, including John Jacob Astor and Benjamin Guggenheim, both prominent businessmen.

Although the Titanic's fate was a catastrophe that scarred a generation, it did not signal the end of the age of shipping. It would be the advances in air travel that finally put sea crossings into the commercial shade. Wilbur and Orville Wright claimed 120 ft of history when they achieved powered flight in North Carolina in 1903. The feat ignited the imagination of engineers across the globe and the science of flight accelerated at an astonishing rate. By 1909 a plane had flown the English Channel, and in 1927 American aviator Charles Lindbergh won a colossal cash prize for being the first to fly across the Atlantic. By the time Lindbergh landed in France, he had been airborne for more than 33 hours. Passenger flights began on a regular basis during the 1930s, slashing journey times just as trains had a century previously.

Aerial technology was soon exploited for the purposes of war. The Prussian Count Ferdinand von Zeppelin (1838–1917) created an airship that flew commercially for the first time in 1910. It was not dissimilar in concept to hot-air balloons, which had been used during the Franco-Prussian war. But Zeppelins, as they were known, were motor-powered and had a greater range. Inevitably, on the outbreak of the First World War, they became used for weapon delivery. Towns on the east coast of England and even London were bombed by Zeppelins. However, the British were able to exploit the airship's biggest weakness. Highly flammable, more than 40 were shot down over London.

Quickly it became clear that the future of aerial warfare lay in aeroplanes rather than airships. Technology was racing ahead, given that the early automatic pistol that killed Archduke Franz Ferdinand in 1914 was fired just a shade over a decade after the first powered flight. Aircraft were used in combat for the first time by Italians against Ottoman positions in North Africa in 1911, when bombs were dropped over the side onto the enemy.

However, the main military virtue of aircraft was believed to be reconnaissance, especially at the start of the conflict. Planes were fitted with two seats so that a pilot might steer a photographer across enemy lines to capture current positions.

Of course, weapons were quickly modified for use by planes and within a couple of years aerial combat became the norm. The most successful pilot of the First World War was Baron Manfred von Richthofen (1892–1918), who, before his own death near the River Somme, notched up 80 'kills', more than half of which were reconnaissance aircraft, barely primed for combat. The leading war ace in the RNAS was Raymond Collishaw with 60 victories.

four

THE GREAT WAR BEGINS

THE WEEKEND THAT WAR broke out I was in Brighton enjoying a bank holiday with my mother. [After the Bank Holidays Act of 1871, the first Monday of August was declared a holiday. The date was changed to the end of August 100 years later.]

We went by train from Victoria Station and it was a complete break for both of us. By this time, aged 18, I was living in lodgings in Bethnal Green. Hundreds of people were enjoying seaside breaks forgetting about work and just relaxing. But the holiday was overshadowed by the talk of war which was rife up and down the country – certainly in London. Newspapers had predicted the conflict for several weeks. When Germany declared war on France on bank holiday Monday, it seemed only a matter of time before Britain would join in. With the grim news, families rushed home from their holiday outings, mingling with troops from the territorial regiments who had been called to the colours. One of my fellow veterans, Donald Hodge, set off to go to France for the day only to find the planned excursion had been cancelled.

'What silly old fool would start a war on a bank holiday?' he asked. Plenty, I thought.

On Tuesday I went back to work and found the streets thronged with people waiting for news – it seemed exciting, yet one was still filled with a dread and the future was unknown. Thousands of men were volunteering in London, and you could see them every day marching off to the enlistment offices. Finally, after Germany invaded Belgium, Britain declared war and it was all over the newspapers.

Shortly before 11 a.m. on 28 June 1914, Archduke Franz Ferdinand, heir to the Austro-Hungarian throne, was shot dead alongside his wife, Sophie, as they travelled through the streets of Sarajevo in Bosnia in a open motorcade. Their assassin was student Gavrilo Princip, an idealist belonging to a group called The Black Hand *who were seeking independence for Serbo-Croats. But Europe had been a pressure cooker for several years and it had taken more than one shot to start a war.*

As early as 1912, Britain withdrew battleships from the Mediterranean Sea in order that they could better patrol the North Sea, in response to the German naval build-up. In the same year it was reported that France spent the most per head of population on arms, followed by Germany, Britain and the United States.

The Ottoman Empire had for centuries ruled vast swathes of the Near and Middle East as well as tracts of southern Europe. However, it was unable to control its rangy empire but unwilling to relinquish the reins. In 1912 the Bulgarians, with the help of Serbian and Greek allies, fell about Ottoman troops in a bid to win independence. When the Turkish capital, Constantinople, was threatened, the Sultan offered peace talks.

The Balkans was under the control of the Austro-Hungarian empire and in the shadow of both the Turkish and Russian empires but had many factions seeking nationhood. Indeed, there had been two short wars in the Balkans in the two years before the outbreak of the First World War, in which first Turkey and then Bulgaria had been defeated by small but ambitious neighbours.

Germany had promised to support its neighbour, Austro-Hungary, especially if Russia mobilised in support of the Serbian Slavs, who were cultural kinfolk. Russia was by now linked through treaties to France which, for its part, had struck up an entente cordiale with Britain.

Turkey had strong military links with Germany as did Bulgaria, while Italy saw its interests best served by an alliance with France and Britain. Thus Europe fell into two rival camps. People in Britain, however, were initially not sure about the wisdom of a war.

After the Archduke's assassination, Austria delivered an ultimatum to Serbia and finally declared war on 28 July. The following week Germany declared war on Russia and France and invaded Belgium. The British people felt for the Belgians – but strategically Britain could not afford Belgian ports to fall into the hands of the growing Imperial German Navy – and so began the mass rallying to the flag. The British declaration of war on Germany, who was now fighting on two fronts, followed. Britain, France and Russia finally declared war on Turkey in November 1914 after the bombardment of Odessa. Italy held off until May 1915, when it declared war on Austro-Hungary. It wasn't until 14 months later that Italy made its declaration of hostilities against Germany. Henry, like all other young men watching international events unfold from afar, was oblivious to the dangers of modern warfare. The excitement of leaving their mundane lives to enlist for foreign adventure was too great a temptation to resist.

The next day I got out my Triumph TT motorcycle and headed for Pall Mall. Not a lot of people could afford a motorbike. It had cost me 20 guineas and I knew you had to have your own to enlist as a dispatch rider.

In Pall Mall the army recruiters were at work. Scores of cheerful volunteers were heading that way. We were all full of patriotism, willing to fight for King and country. Anyone you spoke to wanted to join up and fight the Germans. There was also the sense of adventure and believing we were in an exciting time. But remember that community spirit was also strong at the time – people were born, grew up and died in their own local areas, some not going more than a few miles from their homes in their whole lives. Churches, clubs and societies all responded to the call to arms. For others less fortunate than me it was a way out of a dead-end job and a wasted life. Then family and friends started putting on pressure.

I offered to be a dispatch rider for the Royal Engineers, using my own machine. After queuing for more than half an hour, a sergeant took particulars of myself and my motorbike. Indeed, he seemed more interested in the machine than me. I was told to return home and wait for further instructions.

In fact, the next set of instructions I got was from my mother. She was quite distressed when she heard what I had done and made me promise never to leave her side. In the end it didn't matter. I never heard from the army again. I was asked at least three times to join the Territorial Army but I was too busy. Like everyone else, I hoped the war would be over by Christmas.

Think of the First World War and one image springs to mind, that of Lord Horatio Herbert Kitchener (1850–1916) Secretary of State For War, pointing a finger at a generation of young men, urging them into the battlefields. A series of posters featured a picture of Kitchener with his handlebar moustache and peaked military cap and the words 'Join your country's army' or 'Britons, your country needs you'. Each one was punctuated with the line 'God save the King'. On 6 August 1914, Kitchener persuaded Parliament to authorise the recruitment of 500,000 men, and such was the rush to join up, the quota was filled by the end of September.

It is perhaps one of the most successful advertising campaigns ever conceived. The posters played no small part in prompting three million men to volunteer in the first two years of the war. This in turn meant the politically unpopular topic of conscription could be placed firmly on the back burner by Parliament, despite the massive loss of life in the fields of Flanders. And Britain was sorely short of soldiers.

At the outbreak of war, the regular army had some 247,000 men in 84 infantry battalions at home and 73 battalions overseas, especially in India. There was also a reserve army of some 200,000. Mobilisation had to be effective and fast. On 15 August 1914 about 80,000 men in a newly gathered British Expeditionary Force (BEF) landed in France. Facing them was a German Army of over 1.5 million men, fully trained and ready to mobilise and with a highly rehearsed plan of attack – to knock Britain and France out of the war quickly and decisively.

It is probably true to say that the British people were not ready for war, a modern war fought against another industrial nation such as Germany. The British Army was woefully small in comparison with those of other European countries. Frank Sumpter, one of the veterans, was stationed on the Afghan borders. In the late spring of 1914 his regiment was recalled. Everyone was overjoyed, he said. The men had only been in India for six months and were well pleased to see the back of this region's inhospitable terrain, challenging climate and the dangers of local tribesmen. At first Frank thought it was a hoax, but sure enough they were soon on a troop ship bound for dear old Blighty.

You can imagine the men's disappointment when the ship docked at a port in France. They disembarked from the ship and were told they were part of the British Expeditionary Force. The defence of Mons and the subsequent hell that Frank and the *Old Contemptibles* (troops already serving before the war) suffered during the retreat made India seem like heaven.

As seen on page 41, as a result of the failures the British Army suffered in the Boer War, every soldier was issued with a .303 calibre Lee-Enfield rifle with its ten-round magazine, even those in the cavalry. The only exceptions were among the medical fraternity. Each soldier was made to understand that this was *his* rifle and would stay with him throughout his service. Every rifle had to be zeroed to the soldier personally. The British soldier spent more time on the rifle range than his counterparts in other European armies. In 1914 the BEF rightly earned the reputation of rapid, accurate fire that was second to none.

Back on the home front, Kitchener was the ideal man for the task of stirring national pride. Made Minister of War in 1914 – the first military man to ever hold the post – he was something of a national hero. It was Kitchener who had secured British interests in northern Africa in the Battle of Omdurman in 1898. Indifferent conduct during the Boer War had not diminished this glittering image, although involvement in the unpopular Gallipoli campaign of the First World War did finally dent the public's perception of him.

Kitchener died during a mission to Russia intended to rally support for the war, when HMS Hampshire ran into a mine. Rumours were the mine had been planted by a U-boat, but this has since been discounted in favour of a rogue mine the ship was unfortunate enough to run into. Out of the 655 aboard, only 11 survived and Kitchener's body was never found.

Conspiracy theorists believe Kitchener was assassinated rather than a victim of war. He was certainly falling from grace, not least because the First World War battle campaigns were so cumbersome and his high profile was attached to them. As an army man from his days observing the Franco-Prussian war of 1870, he found politicians difficult to work with and gathered more than a few enemies.

THE GRANDMOTHER OF EUROPE
Henry Allingham was five years old when Queen Victoria died in 1901.
She is still the longest serving British monarch to date.

REGISTRATION DISTRICT   Hackney

1896   BIRTH in the Sub-district of Stamford Hill   in the   County of London

Columns:-	1	2	3	4	5	6	7	8	9	10
No.	When and where born	Name, if any	Sex	Name and surname of father	Name, surname and maiden surname of mother	Occupation of father	Signature, description and residence of informant	When registered	Signature of registrar	Name entered after registration
55	Tenth June 1896 2 Eden Terrace Harrington Hill upper Clapton	Henry	Boy	Henry Thomas Allingham	Amy Jane Allingham formerly Foster	Mercantile Clerk	H. J. Allingham Father 2 Eden Terrace Harrington Hill upper Clapton	Twenty Seventh June 1896	A. Jones Registrar	

CERTIFIED to be a true copy of an entry in the certified copy of a Register of Births in the District above mentioned.

Given at the GENERAL REGISTER OFFICE, under the Seal of the said Office, the _____ 10th _____ day of _____ September _____ 2007

BXCC 691200

HENRY ON THE RECORDS
A copy of Henry's birth certificate showing his arrival as the year 1896.

HENRY ON THE RECORDS
This 1900 census records Henry living with his mother and grandparents in Walthamstow in London. He is fifth from the top of the list.

PUBLIC RECORD OFFICE   REFERENCE :-   **RG 13/1623**   CROWN COPYRIGHT · NOT TO BE REPRODUCED WITHOUT PERMISSION

HENRY'S PARENTS
His father tragically died of tuberculosis within
three years of Henry's birth.

THE INFANT HENRY
Hard to believe this was taken 112 years ago
and the subject is still here to look at it.

AT THE SEASIDE
A young Henry excited about being at the
seaside with his grandparents in Cromer – scene
of the infamous 'teapot' incident.

THE GRANDPARENTS
Henry's beloved grandparents who took
Henry and his mother in once his father had
died so young at the age of 26.

EDWARD VII'S CORONATION
Henry was with his family celebrating the King's coronation in 1901 and actually
witnessed the King's carriage passing by.

THE BIRTH OF THE MOTORCAR
Henry can still recall seeing his first car – travelling at 4 mph – in 1900. It would have looked
fairly similar to this Peugeot of the same period.

THE TEENAGE HENRY
A 14 year old who loved the outdoors, especially cricket. He watched WG Grace play for Surrey.

ALMOST A MAN
A youthful Henry Allingham, starting to think about what he'll do as a career once his schooling has finished.

ON THE RIVER
Henry loved anything to do with the water – as seen here where he is rowing in the bowman's birth on the Thames.

THE GREAT WAR BEGINS
The passion to fight for one's country drove hundreds of thousands of men to enlist upon Britain's declaration of war in the summer of 1914.

HENRY ENLISTS
By 1915, and with his mother dead, Henry was free to enlist and fight. He joined the Royal Naval Air Service.

THE RNAS CREW
On an outing in a naval car with a collection of his fellow recruits, Henry is sitting in the front seat, depicted by the cross above his head.

SET FOR WAR ON A HORSE
Henry larking around at home with one of his chums in the RNAS whilst on leave.

THE BIRTH OF TERROR WEAPONS
A German Zeppelin L53, taken out of its shed, of the kind used by the German air force for reconnaissance and bombing missions over the British Isles.

THE RNAS IN ACTION, 1917
A squadron of Avro bombers – that would have been flown in Henry's unit – lined up and ready to take-off on their mission. The RNAS was the backbone of many British air offensives on the Western Front.

HENRY'S PLANE
The British BE2c was the workhorse of the RNAS and Henry serviced these aircraft, as well as going on many sorties with the pilots – armed with basic hand bombs and a Lee Enfield .303 rifle.

THE BATTLE OF JUTLAND, 1916
Henry's ship was part of the British Grand Fleet that thwarted German plans of dominating the high seas – though Britain lost a great deal more men and ships in the battle.

KING GEORGE V VISITS THE FRONT LINE
The King felt very dearly the cost of executing the Great War and continually ventured over to France to meet his generals and see for himself what was going on – as here in 1917.

THE COST OF WAR
What is left of the once beautiful town of Ypres after the third battle in 1917, where Henry fought as part of the air offensive to support the infantry assaults.

HAIL THE GLORIOUS DEAD
The tomb of the Unknown Warrior laid to rest amongst the kings and queens of England in Westminster in 1920.

However, history has judged him more kindly. He correctly predicted a long and costly war when others were insisting it would be over by Christmas. He was the unlikely innovator of a new knitted-sock pattern that did away with seams that could prove painful for soldiers. Also, a week before his death, he declared the necessity for a peace of reconciliation, in the same way he proved to be the voice of reason following the Boer War. For those who insist the punitive measures of the Versailles Treaty that ended the First World War instigated the second global conflict in 1939, then Kitchener's death assumes the gravity of an international tragedy.

In 1916 hoaxer Frank Power claimed to have recovered Kitchener's body and a funeral at St Paul's Cathedral was planned. However, suspicious officials opened the coffin to discover it was filled with tar rather than the remains of the great strategist. Charges were never laid against Power, however, and speculation about the fate of Kitchener continued.

A week after war was declared, I lost my job. Gordon's saw just about all its workers disappear into Kitchener's volunteer army. So I joined Scammell's, the truck manufacturer, working long hours, sometimes all through the night. My job was to modify Foden and Scammell trucks to army specifications. Mostly my life consisted of bed and work.

I got news about the war from the newspapers. We all believed that the people knew only half of what was happening in Flanders, the press knew three quarters and only the government knew the full story – and ministers weren't saying anything. Casualty lists were not published until May 1915. However, I can remember *The Times* publishing an article in late November 1914 that included the phrase: 'Day after day the butchery of the unknown by the unseen. At a cost of thousands of lives a few hundred yards may be gained.'

Years later Dennis told me about the fate of the British Expeditionary Force at Mons. Apparently, 80,000 BEF men were marched towards Mauberge to link up with the French Army. Following German successes against the French at Sambre and Mamur, the French Army decided to retreat, leaving the BEF well forward. On 22 August 1914 the BEF soldiers were deployed along a 20-mile front, digging deep trenches and taking advantage of the many slag heaps from the nearby mines – perfect cover. Every building was turned into a fortress. The advancing Germans looking towards the canal could see no sign of their enemy. Ultimately the British repulsed the advance and inflicted severe casualties with pin-point artillery and rapid fire from the infantry. This was the first full-scale attack of the war and the British had delivered a bloody nose to the other side. The advancing Germans believed they were facing machine guns such was the rate of accurate firepower from the disciplined British troops who unleashed their rapid bolt action fire drilled into them during many hours of training.

Almost immediately, though, the British – in the absence of reinforcements – were compelled to pull back. A marching and fighting retreat for the next 14 days brought the soldiers to the outskirts of Paris. Between 24 August and 5 September some 15,000 BEF men were killed, wounded or missing. Both sides continued to mount offensives but neither gained much ground. By Christmas 1914 the butcher's bill for the BEF was just under 90,000 – roughly the same number of men that initially landed in France in August. On average, one officer and 30 men survived in each battalion. This was a real shock to the nation as losses on this scale had never happened in their experience, and even during the Boer Wars the Army hadn't suffered anything like these casualty figures. It opened people's eyes to what was coming, certainly the war wouldn't be over by Christmas!

Had the British Expeditionary Force failed, the course of the war would have been different. All young men of fighting age would have been called up immediately, including Henry, to defend the shores of Kent and Sussex. So it was the BEF's heroic actions that enabled Henry's life to unfold as it did. Mons is rightly seen as the first of many heroic and costly actions by the British Army in the Great War. It was the Kaiser himself who labelled the BEF 'Contemptibles' due to the insignificant strength compared to his formidable forces. Henry himself heard the story that the German Naval Command asked the military if they would desire the German Navy to attack British shipping in the English Channel to prevent the BEF reaching French soil. It was decided by German HQ to allow them to cross unmolested as the sooner they reached France, the sooner they could be destroyed! This was the thinking at the time that the German Army was too strong for such a tiny force as the BEF and they would not put up any long-term obstruction to a German march to the sea to capture the Channel ports.

Sometimes I would have a meal at Lyon's Corner House with my family or enjoy a trip to the theatre. The shows at the Gaiety Theatre included 'England Expects' and 'Tonight's the Night'. I went with my Mother, Nanna or Auntie Rosie – they were the only women I knew. But, as I wasn't in uniform, I ran the risk of being confronted by outraged women who had taken to shaming men into enlistment by presenting them with a white feather, a sign of cowardice.

Women were under enormous pressure to lend support to Kitchener's campaign for volunteers. General poster campaigns were numerous, like the picture of John Bull in his Union Jack waistcoat asking: 'Who's absent – is it you?' There was a drawing of a man with children on his knee asking: 'Daddy, what did you do in the Great War?' And some were especially designed to appeal to women. 'Women of Britain, say "Go"' prompted women to persuade their menfolk to join up. 'Is your best boy wearing khaki? Don't you think he should be?' was another. Also, one warned: 'If your young man neglects his duty to King and country, the time may come when he will neglect you.'

I was never accosted in the street but I know plenty of men who were. In the theatre, Vesta Tilly (1864–1952), a male impersonator best remembered for the song 'Burlington Bertie', dressed in uniform and sang recruitment songs including 'Jolly Good Luck to the Girl Who Loves a Soldier'.

In July 1915 the National Registration Bill was passed, making it compulsory to register your personal details with the government so they could tell who was working where. Although they denied it, the government was obviously thinking in terms of conscription. [Compulsory military service was introduced in January 1916.]

I had been bound by the promise I made to my mother not to get involved as I was her only child. But in June 1915 my mother died of cancer. Before her death she gave me a diamond ring engraved with the words 'Mother to Henry 1915'. She must have done that when she knew she was dying. With her death I was released from my pledge not to volunteer and now I quickly enquired about joining up. Everyone I knew had done so already, and one could see whole bodies of men forming up the 'Pals Battalions' – later to be slaughtered in 1916. Cheshire produced 24 local battalions including the Accrington Pals – 585 men out of 700 who enlisted perished on the Somme. My local football team Clapton Orient (later changed to Leyton Orient) had the distinction of having the largest number of recruits from a single club – 41 men, most of whom were killed or wounded.

I'd gone off the idea of being a dispatch rider, but the community feeling of patriotism and the prospect of adventure was still there.

A new interest was sparked one Sunday afternoon when I was riding my pedal bike in the countryside near Chingford, Essex, near a reservoir. I heard a droning noise and looked up to see a plane circling the aerodrome. It was a captivating sight.

Fascinated, I sat down on the grass verge to watch the aircraft. I decided that was for me so I vowed to apply to join the Royal Naval Air Service. Much later Dennis told me about an obscure but prophetic poem by Thomas Gray (1716–1771), author of the famous *Elegy Written in a Country Churchyard*. It fitted how I felt that day.

> The time will come when thou shalt lift thine eyes
> To watch a long drawn battle in the skies
> While aged peasants, too amazed for words
> Stare at the flying fleets of wond'rous birds.
> England so long the mistress of the seas,
> Where winds and waves confess her sovereignty
> Her ancient triumph yet on high shall bear
> And reign, the sovereign of the conquered air.

What did Henry know about the RNAS? Not a great deal. He was older than the service he was going to join. IOn 13 May 1912 it was decided to have two wings in the British Armed Forces, one military and one naval. The Royal Flying Corps (RFC) was consequently formed, alongside the Naval Wing. In addition there was to be a Central Flying School. Command of the military wing was given to Captain F.H. Sykes, his rank perhaps underlying the relative unimportance given to this new organization at that time. The Royal Navy – being the senior service – on the other hand, asserted its independence by unofficially calling itself the Royal Naval Air Service (RNAS). In August 1913 Brigadier General Sir David Henderson was appointed the Military Aeronautics Directorate at the War Office. The British Navy was allocated army airships and 12 aircraft to be used in conjunction with its ships. The first flight from a moving ship took place in May 1912. The following year, the first seaplane carrier, Hermes, was commissioned, and one can see the rush to re-arm for aerial warfare was a priority by reading this speech by Winston Churchill – who was to be the First Sea Lord during the war – given at the Lord Mayor's banquet in 1913. Henry believes it was Churchill himself who helped create the RNAS.

Even in the region of the air, into which with characteristic British prudence we have moved with some tardiness, the Navy need not fear comparison with the Navy of any other country. The British sea-plane, although still in an empirical stage, like everything else in this sphere of warlike operations, has reached a point of progress in advance of anything attained elsewhere.

Our hearts should go out tonight to those brilliant officers, Commander Samson [the first man to take off from a ship in 1911 – HMS *Africa*] and his band of brilliant pioneers, to whose endeavours, to whose enterprise, to whose devotion it is due that in an incredibly short space of time our naval aeroplane service has been raised to that primacy from which it must never be cast down.

It is not only in naval hydroplanes that we must have superiority. The enduring safety of this country will not be maintained by force of arms unless over the whole sphere of aerial development we are able to make ourselves the first nation. That will be a task of long duration. Many difficulties have to be overcome. Other countries have started sooner. The native genius of France, the indomitable perseverance of Germany, have produced results which we at the present time cannot equal.

The Navy also began to build a chain of coastal air stations and in January 1914 the government established the Royal Naval Air Service (RNAS).

At the outbreak of war, the RNAS had a force of 93 aeroplanes and seaplanes – more than the RFC – and a complement of 100 officers and 550 ratings spread among six naval air stations. In 1914 the RNAS undertook responsibility for the air defence of Great Britain. The RNAS was primarily concerned with seeking out enemy shipping and harassing intruder submarines. It also repelled invaders and protected the British coastline.

At first its seaplanes were unable to land or take off from ships so, instead, they were hoisted into or out of the water by cranes. A few ships were then modified so that there could be take-offs from the deck. Planes such as the Sopwith Pup, which was exceptionally nimble, were suited for this purpose. But it wasn't until 1918 and the modification of HMS Argus *that an aircraft carrier from which planes could both take off and land was in service. The RNAS quickly set up a base in Dunkirk at the outset of war to combat the threat of the dreaded Zeppelin attacks expected on UK shores.*

five

HENRY VOLUNTEERS

IN SEPTEMBER 1915 THE RNAS contacted me for the first time, asking me to take a medical. I had to report to a gym at Admiralty Arch in London. I was nervous and skipped breakfast, having just a glass of water beforehand. I knew there would be a series of physical examinations to prove our fitness, where I was examined from head to toe.

There were 16 of us and we were told to jump onto parallel bars while the naval surgeon walked along the line. Unfortunately I was last in line and gritted my teeth as I began to feel the strain. I was almost ready to drop when the surgeon, with hands like hams, prodded me and said: 'You're in.'

I dropped to the floor, relieved that I hadn't fallen off in front of everyone. At four o'clock I ate my first meal of the day and I was starving. Then I discovered that I had to take a series of aptitude tests before I could become a mechanic. I was sent to Sheerness in Kent for assessment.

I was joined there by 14 other hopefuls, including two Americans, two Australians and two New Zealanders. That first night we were each given two blankets and told to sleep on the floor of a hut. Instantly, I didn't feel I was going to like this as a career. But the next morning we were allocated beds. And, although the first week was boring, the remaining three weeks at the camp were a real challenge. We did written and practical tests. I felt that in some areas of maintenance, the RNAS was not as advanced as its engineering equivalents in civvy street.

I successfully completed the course and on 21 September 1915 I was given a number (RNAS F8317) and rank (Air Mechanic Second Class). I was asked which station I would like to be posted into and I replied, 'East Africa.' I had heard about the adventures of an expeditionary squadron of 20 officers and men from the RNAS who had taken two Sopwith Type 807 seaplanes to East Africa in January 1915, hunting for the German ship the *Königsberg*.

The story of the Königsberg *reads like a* Boy's Own *adventure and began before the war when the German government decided to post a modern cruiser to their East African colony – seen as a key component of their colonial policy. It would enhance the status of German East Africa with its capital of Dar es Salaam, and reinforce the German Navy's ability to conduct commerce warfare in the case of a major conflict with European powers – specifically Britain and France. This last item was not lost on Great Britain, which was keenly aware of the German colony's proximity to major shipping routes.*

In 1913 Captain Max Looff was assigned to command a hand-picked crew reliable for not only their skill on board ship, but also their stability and temperament, as the journey would be long, and tropical stations required unusual stamina. With the outbreak of war in the summer of 1914, by 30 July the ship was ready and armed to take the war to the high seas. Fortunately escaping three British cruisers in bad weather that had been sent to destroy her, she was now free to wreak havoc in the Indian Ocean.

Six nights later, Königsberg *was pushing her way through heavy seas off Cape Guardafui when she received the long anticipated order:* EGIMA, *the code word meaning that Germany was now at war with Great Britain, France and Russia. In all the long miles of the Indian Ocean,* Königsberg *was now alone and being hunted by the Allied navies. But she herself was built and armed to be a hunter, and Captain Looff desired to locate and destroy British shipping as quickly as possible. The British steamer* City of Winchester *was her first prize, the* Königsberg *taking her coal and then scuttling her after a few days.*

Tacking back and forward over the next several months, Königsberg *would cause havoc to British interests as she destroyed shipping, attacked and sunk the cruiser* Pegasus *in the British naval base at Zanzibar, and led a merry chase to a squadron of British warships. Eventually, with a damaged piston shaft and trapped in the Rufiji delta along the East African coast, the captain and crew – together with a local German garrison – dug entrenchments and unloaded light armaments from the ship. They would carry on the war and hope to be resupplied and refit the ship. To the British the ship was still a major danger to Allied shipping as they did not know the extent to which she was disabled – she still had to be destroyed. Despite various British naval blockades, aerial bombardments and attacks by smaller vessels who could navigate the shallower channels, it would not be until a full-scale coordinated attack in July 1915 that the ship would be sunk. Even then, the majority of the crew escaped, unloaded the main guns of the ship and carried on the war on land until 1918. This was a massive propaganda coup for the Germans as they sought to take on and defeat the might of the British Navy.*

But instead of East Africa I got sent to the east coast. I was posted to the Royal Naval Air Station in Great Yarmouth from where the RNAS patrolled coastal waters and safeguarded shipping from German submarines. It also had to contend with the threat of Zeppelins.

The first airship raids were approved by the Kaiser in January 1915, although his honour and blood-line connections to George V made him demand that no attacks be made on historic or government buildings or museums – and undertaken by the German Navy. Attacking at nighttime for protection from roving fighters, military sites were the only targets at the time, but after blackouts became widespread, many bombs fell randomly in East Anglia.

The very first raid was on 19 January 1915, the first bombing of British civilians ever, in which two Zeppelins dropped high-explosive bombs and ineffective incendiaries on Great Yarmouth, Sheringham, King's Lynn and the surrounding villages. In all four people were killed, sixteen injured although the reaction by the British press was out of all proportion to the death toll and damage to property. There were a further 19 raids in 1915, killing 181 people and injuring 455. British defences were divided between the Royal Navy and the British Army at first, before the Army took full control in February 1916. Aerial defences against Zeppelins were haphazard and the lack of an interrupter gear in early fighters meant the basic technique of downing them was to drop bombs on them. The first man to bring down a Zeppelin in this way was R.A.J. Warneford of the RNAS, flying a Morane Parasol on 7 June 1915. Dropping six 9 kg bombs, he set fire to LZ 37 over Ghent and as a result won the Victoria Cross.

Raids continued in 1916. After an accidental bombing of London in May, by July of that year the Kaiser allowed directed raids against urban centres. There were a further 23 airship raids in 1916, killing 293 people and injuring 691. Anti-aircraft defences were becoming tougher and new Zeppelins were introduced which increased their operating altitude from 1,800 to 3,750 metres (5,900 to 12,000 ft). To avoid searchlights, they flew above the clouds whenever possible, lowering an observer through them to direct the bombing. The improved safety was counteracted by the extra strain on the airship crews and the British introduction in mid-1916 of synchronised-gun fighters. The first night-fighter victory came *on 2 September 1916 when Lt William Leefe Robinson, flying from Sutton's Farm, shot down one of a 16-strong raiding force over London, using incendiary ammunition. (The airship was not a Zeppelin but a wooden-framed Schütte-Lanz SL11.) He too was awarded a Victoria Cross. Early in the morning of 24 September 1916, an airborne fighter and anti-aircraft guns caused the L.33 (*Kapitänleutnant Bocker*) to crash land at Little Wigborough near Colchester, Essex, on its first raid. A close inspection of its wrecked structure enabled the British to understand where their own rigid airship designs had been deficient.*

Effective fighters marked the end of the Zeppelin threat. New Zeppelins came into service that could operate at 5,500 metres (18,000 ft) but exposed them to extremes of cold, and changeable winds that could, and did, scatter many Zeppelin raids. In 1917 and 1918 there were only 11 Zeppelin raids against England, the final one on 5 August 1918.

Fifty-one raids were undertaken during the war across London and South-east England, in which 5,806 bombs were dropped, killing 557 people and injuring 1,358. It has been argued the raids were far more effective as terror weapons on the civilian population of Britain. Beyond material damage these raids diverted and disrupted wartime production, and caused the redeployment of 12 fighter squadrons and over 10,000 personnel to air defences. Henry himself would see a Zeppelin attack over London.

At the start of the war, planes were no more than motorised kites. They were flimsy constructions of wood, fabric and wire, powered by an engine less powerful than the present-day car. The instrument panel had six dials. There was a joystick and a rudder bar. To say that they were unreliable is putting it mildly. Although I had no input on design, I did carry out some modifications, replacing the locknuts with my own 'specials', which I had made and knew would be safer.

My first CO was the famous Charles Rummey Samson – the first British pilot to take off from a ship in 1912. I served under him in the armoured car sections for six weeks. One squadron commander I also served under, W.P.C. de Courcy Ireland, was killed in an airship test on 21 February 1916. He was replaced by Lieutenant Commander Douglas Oliver, who was famous for taking part in the first-ever raid by seaplanes, which took place on Christmas morning 1914. The target was a Zeppelin hangar in Cuxhaven, Germany. Nine aircraft were transported as near to the coast as possible by the ships *Engadine, Riviera* and *Empress,* former cross-channel ferry boats that had been converted to carry seaplanes. Only seven aircraft managed to get airborne. The mission wasn't a great success, hampered by fog and lack of experience. Although bomb damage to the hangar was reported by the Germans, this must have happened by accident as none of the pilots were aware of being close to their target. They ditched their three 20-lb bombs over the side to save fuel for the return journey, not knowing which part of Germany they were above. Only two managed to return to their carriers while the rest ditched in the sea. Submarine E11 managed to rescue the crews.

Everyone acquired a nickname and mine was 'Ally'. Lt Commander Douglas Oliver's was 'Snakey', a reference to his long, lean figure. I watched his single-handed attack on German battle cruisers shelling Great Yarmouth, for which he was awarded the Distinguished Service Order. One shell had hit the fish market sheds, causing a terrible stink.

Snakey did a lot to break down the barriers that always existed between officers and men. I can remember when new ratings were trying to recover a plane from the sea at Great Yarmouth, with some difficulty. Snakey arrived on the scene and was outraged to see a group of newly commissioned officers watching events from the slipway. He ordered the officers in their new uniforms to wade in and help. Their pride was severely dented.

Another incident that made me laugh at the time was when three Australians from the Great Yarmouth station walked past a Royal Navy officer without saluting. The officer called them back stiffly and asked, 'Do you know who I am?'

'No idea, cobber,' came the reply.

'I'm in charge . . . '

'Good on yer, mate. You've got yourself a good number, I shouldn't complain. See you around.'

The Australians went on their way and, if Snakey had got to hear of the exchange, I doubt they would have got into trouble. In that way the men of the RNAS were a new breed.

When I joined up lots of people doubted that air power would ever be any use. Even Field Marshal Douglas Haig thought its only purpose was for reconnaissance. From our first day, we set out to prove the doubters wrong.

I was involved in everything from repairing and maintaining the aircraft, pulling up seaplanes from the water's edge and helping night landings by using rows of flares to light up the runway.

My first flight was in 1915, just a dozen years after Orville Wright's first-ever powered flight. I remember it like it was yesterday. I was the engineer in an Avro 504 biplane flying on a routine patrol over the North Sea. I always wore long johns, they were standard issue. But this time I put on as many clothes as I could find, covering the lot with my RNAS issue tunic with patch pockets.

If it was available, you'd smear Vaseline on your face to protect it from the cold weather. If that wasn't available, then it was whale oil or engine grease because you were flying in an open cockpit with only a small windshield for protection. You wore gloves to protect you from frostbite. It was so noisy, I do remember the deafening throb and the chap on the ground shouting, 'Chocks away!' Then we were up, the freezing wind gushing past my face as we climbed steeply, my heart in my stomach as we banked. It was a great adventure for a bloke like me.

The Avro biplane came into service before the war. It was a sturdy little plane but I still felt a bit queasy. It was sometimes the worst type of plane to fly, lacking speed through lack of power. Watching from the ground, I had seen an Avro in the air start to go backwards when a strong easterly gust was blowing. The engine just couldn't cope with those conditions.

We had just enough fuel to get us to the Dutch coast and back again. I took with me a Lee-Enfield rifle and two carrier pigeons. There was no method of communication in planes at the time. Radio came later. So the homing pigeons, by returning to base, acted as a signal for help and could even take coordinates in a message strapped to their legs if time allowed.

I knew of a Curtis seaplane that had ditched in the North Sea. The crew hadn't taken pigeons and they had no means of signalling for help. They drifted on the sea for five days, drinking water from the plane's radiator. Navy ships in the area began a search and by luck a destroyer on patrol found them bobbing in the sea just moments before the ship started heading for home.

The first thing I did in a plane was to listen to the pitch of the engine. That would tell me if anything was wrong – whether we should abandon the mission before we started. To be honest, all the planes were so flimsy and unpredictable – as well as incapable of carrying large fuel loads – at the start of the war that both British and German pilots would immediately turn back rather than face each other in the skies if they did not enjoy height supremacy. But I remember getting back on the ground and just itching to take off again.

Pilots and observers led a precarious existence, with safety measures at a bare minimum. Despite the fact that parachutes had been invented prior to the start of the war, none were issued to British pilots.

Admittedly, the 'Guardian Angel' parachute developed by railway engineer E.R. Calthrop (1857–1927) weighed a hefty 90 lb and was impossible to stow on early aircraft. Calthrop went back to the drawing board and designed another parachute weighing just 24 lb. He was so convinced by his design that in 1915 he ran trials for the RFC and RNAS top brass to convince them of its worth. However, a report pouring rain on his parade was issued, claiming 'the presence of a parachute might impair the fighting spirit of pilots and cause them to abandon machines which might otherwise be capable of returning to base for repair'. Calthrop, who had spent £12,000 on research, was encouraged to stay silent about the potential of parachutes, although they were used to drop agents behind enemy lines. Parachutes were also issued to pilots from Germany, France and America.

Outraged by the number of pilots being killed on the Western Front, Calthrop finally spoke out about his invention and won the support of pilots in the field. In August 1918 an order was issued, stating that all aeroplanes should be equipped with parachutes. The Armistice brought the scheme to a halt. In 1916 Calthrop also invented an ejector seat for pilots, working on compressed air.

Anyone involved in flying at the time had a dread of fire on landing. Pilots held their hands high as they struggled to escape. I've seen so many men burned up, pals as well. You tried never to get too close to people. They died in a matter of seconds, there was nothing anyone could do. All you could do was stand by helplessly and watch. You would just hope it was quick. We were always told to move away from the aircraft after a flight as quickly as possible and wait for 20 minutes before going near it again.

Crash landings were common. Once I was returning from a patrol with pilot Major Egbert Cadbury. Everything looked all right as we were coming down but as we touched the ground the nose dipped. We lost half the undercarriage and the plane ended up half-buried in the ground. Major Cadbury and I scrambled out quickly. I heard a torrent of expletives from the major that included words I'd never heard before or since. Parachutes had been invented but they were never issued to crews in the RNAS.

Air Commodore Sir Egbert Cadbury (1893–1967) was the grandson of the man who founded the famous confectionary empire. A devout Quaker, John Cadbury first opened for business in Birmingham in 1824, believing chocolate and cocoa an ideal alternative to the evils of alcohol.

John's son George (1839–1922) eventually took over the business and oversaw its move to Bournville, a newly created village comprising the factory and accommodation for its workers. George was also guided by his Quaker beliefs and introduced innovations such as affordable housing, holidays and pensions for Cadbury workers.

When George's son Egbert joined the forces, it was in direct contravention of his family's pacifist Quaker beliefs. At least one of his brothers joined the Friends Ambulance Service, manned by conscientious objectors who nonetheless saw the worst side of war by placing themselves in the front line to help wounded soldiers.

Egbert shot down two Zeppelins, one in 1916 and the other two years later. When he returned to civvy street, Cadbury's was in the midst of a merger with J.S. Fry, another confectionary company run by Quakers, and Egbert joined the Fry's side of the business empire. His son Peter, born in Great Yarmouth in 1918, went on to found Westward Television in the West Country.

I don't know what I would have done if, on my first patrol over the North Sea, I had encountered a German ship. You must remember that all I had in the cockpit was a .303 Lee-Enfield rifle, sometimes two. Even if we'd had bombs aboard, it was pretty futile to pitch a slow-moving aircraft into a hail of fire let loose by a ship. We first got the Lewis gun, a light machine gun, in June 1916. But we had the problem of trying to shoot through the propeller as it went around. Then they developed the synchromesh gear, which sorted out the timing. After 1917 radios were put in aircraft, although they could only send signals over a distance of 40 miles.

I always felt the name Allingham did me no favours at all. It was there at the top of the roll call when it came to looking for volunteers for a job – any job. But that never bothered me as I was always ready to stick my neck out and have a go. I wasn't married or a father so I had nothing to lose, had I?

While I was posted at Great Yarmouth I had to do a bit on the switchboard. Everybody did. I knew the other fellows would sit there chatting up the girls at the exchange. But I never did. I didn't have a sister and I had no idea what to say to girls. They were another nation, so to speak. But one night I decided it was now or never. I carefully arranged all the music records, putting those I imagined to be the newest to the fore. About eight o'clock you'd ring the exchange and ask for a time check. And you'd get the time. Sometimes we'd go on to speak about the weather. This time I said to the girl on the other end: 'Would you like to hear one of our records?'

'I've heard 'em all,' came the reply. That shot me down on my first attempt.

But one Sunday afternoon when I was walking around Great Yarmouth on my first weekend off in a while, I passed the parish church where there was a group of people and I saw Harper, a freckle-faced man from Devon who was my Chief Petty Officer and immediate boss. He was with his wife and another young woman. Harper called me over and I duly went, believing it to be an order. I marched quite briskly towards him in what I hoped was naval style.

'I see that they have given you Sunday off but you are too late for this service,' he said. Everybody laughed but I didn't know what to say. Then after a few minutes of conversation, Harper and his wife left. I knew the woman's name was Dorothy but I didn't know what else to say and the atmosphere was awkward. I knew I was staring. I knew I had to say something, but what?

'Do you live here?' I asked, then felt a fool for asking such a daft question.

But she simply said, 'Yes.'

More silence threatened to nip the relationship in the bud. I asked if I could walk her home and she agreed, saying 'It's not very far.' As we got under way I noticed the chestnut growing in the churchyard.

'What a beautiful tree,' I remarked. 'That tree is probably older than the church.' The tree became special to us and I always looked out for it when I was flying.

Dorothy Cater lived across the River Yar at 10 Anson Road and, in 1916, the ferry cost a halfpenny per crossing. It saved ten minutes' walking so I paid a penny. I discovered Dorothy was a sales assistant in Kerridge Drapers and received commission on sales. When we arrived at her house I asked if I could see her again the following week and she said yes.

Later I asked Dorothy to take a boat ride. I inspected all the craft before saying to the proprietor, 'I'll take that one.' I hoped she was impressed that I knew what I was talking about. We went off down the river to Horning where we stopped for cream buns and strawberries.

Our meetings became more regular. On evenings when it was clear the weather had set in and there was no flying to be done, I decided to go over the wall – to leave the camp for a limited period in the night, which was strictly against regulations. But so long as I was back by reveille, no one would know.

Dorothy lived with her Uncle Fred and Auntie Nellie. Uncle Fred never questioned how much leave I was able to secure. Both of us refrained from talking about matters regarding the air station.

Only much later did I discover that Uncle Fred was in charge of the men who guarded the camp and must have had a good idea that I was breaking the rules.

When I was a child, my Nanna taught me how to play whist. Fortunately, Dorothy, Fred and Nellie all enjoyed playing whist so there was often a battle of the green baize taking place between us at their house. I knew it was time to go home when Uncle Fred would get up and wind the clock. Dorothy saw me off at the garden gate and we made arrangements for our next meeting. We never kissed in the early stages of our relationship.

Things improved when I was offered a chance to live outside the base. I had my own lodgings and the RNAS paid me an allowance. It was a room in Kent Road and the owner was a widow. I used to buy my own food and she cooked for me. I was particularly fond of bloater and often treated myself to one. I got to know the fishermen in Great Yarmouth who landed them, so that frequently I would get the fattest fish available.

There was a dance hall in Great Yarmouth called Caesar's Palace. The proprietor offered free admittance to naval staff, mainly in order to attract lots of girls, who would have to pay to get in and would want dance partners. I enjoyed the waltzes and quicksteps, but singularly failed to take home any of my dance partners. But once I had met Dorothy I didn't go again. She made it clear that she thought it was not a good place to go for either me or her.

The town had a theatre as well and we might have gone there more often if a group of sailors had not set off the emergency hoses in the auditorium when they were drunk one night. After that, servicemen like me were banned.

On 13 April 1916 King George V inspected the air station and its aircraft. I was hugely disappointed when the King, having spoken to many individuals standing in a line, turned and left just before reaching me. I have taken great pleasure in telling Prince Charles when I have met with him that I have seen his great-grandfather in the flesh.

George V was almost a reluctant monarch in 1910 – more famous for staying at home to view his stamp collection than involve himself in state affairs. This would change with the outbreak of war in 1914. With such strong German links to the Kaiser (who was his cousin) as well as still having a German name – Saxe-Coburg-Gotha, the king moved quickly to establish his family firmly in the bosom of the British people. He adopted the name of Windsor for the royal family, encouraged his relations to change their German names for more acceptable anglophile versions, and actively courted public opinion with many visitations and walkabouts so the country could see him and Queen Mary for themselves. He won new respect from his subjects by showing he was with them, not only at home in the factories and dockyards, but also on the front line in France and Flanders – which he visited on several occasions. As the war progressed and the British people suffered deeply from losses on the front line as well as deprivations at home, George V was shrewd enough to know that the mood of the country would not tolerate the Tsar and his family settling in Britain once they had been overthrown in the Russian Revolution of 1917. They would not be the last relatives among European royalty to be forced out of their countries as the war took hold across the continent. Despite a nervous beginning George V's reign has been favourably reviewed by history: his reign not only encompassed the Great War, but also the rebellion and later civil war in Ireland, the rise of nationalism in India and the Great Depression of the 1930s.

six

ACTIVE SERVICE IN THE RNAS

ONE SUNDAY MORNING IN May, when I was on duty in the sheds, I was summoned by senior officers. It was just before lunchtime and I was racking my brains for the reason. The duty petty officer told me to get down to the quay and join HMT *Kingfisher*.

I'd worked on the *Kingfisher* many times before, typically on anti-submarine and anti-Zeppelin patrols that lasted two or three days. I much preferred the *Brocklesbury*, an old paddle steamer used for the same purposes, as the accommodation was better and it didn't smell of fish.

As I got close to the armed trawler I realised it was at the centre of considerable activity. I could see that a Sopwith Schneider was ready for loading. I was pleased it was a Schneider as I considered this plane my baby. I liked working on it and it performed well.

Once I got on board I found out that the vessel was being fitted out for a mission at sea, the destination and duration unknown.

My first response was that I had no kit. I only had what I stood up in. But the crew men were welcoming and I knew they would look after me. The Sopwith pilot, a flight sub lieutenant, was also aboard. HMT *Kingfisher* set sail that evening under sealed orders.

The next day I discovered that we were to rendezvous with the Grand Fleet in the North Sea. The Sopwith Schneider was to be ready for reconnaissance flights. At the time it was an early model and was incapable of long flights. So it was brought to the scene of the action and lowered into the sea from its host ship. In rough weather this was a difficult operation. Nor was the Sopwith particularly effective at its task of detecting and reporting enemy positions, including speed and direction. The plane could not hover, could not fly slowly and was so unsteady that telescopes were useless. When the plane was being lowered or recovered, the ship it travelled on turned into a sitting duck.

The *Kingfisher* eventually joined the Grand Fleet that evening. The entire might of the British Navy steamed past us, going hell for leather. From the deck of the *Kingfisher* I could see three dreadnoughts, cutting through the sea at speed, rising and falling in crashing waves. Cruisers and destroyers followed behind in parallel lines. As night closed in we followed in their wake.

The next day, 31 May 1916, the Battle of Jutland began with us on the periphery, waiting for orders. Really it had been our job to search for Jerry in the Schneider. But we couldn't do much in the dark and the Germans were spotted just before dawn so we never flew. I could see flashes from the guns of the warships and heard the destruction as the British and German navies hurled shells at one another. It was impossible to tell what was going on.

On 1 June the *Kingfisher* came under attack. I was on deck when there was a flash and the sound of thunder as a German warship unleashed its shells. I stood riveted on the deck, shocked by the suddenness of it all. Suddenly I spotted a shell that seemed to be coming straight for me. Fortunately it went straight over the top of the *Kingfisher* and vanished into the depths of the sea. That made me think it was a dud one.

Soon the *Kingfisher* was making its way back to Great Yarmouth, its crew unaware of what had gone on in battle. Only when we heard the church bells ring out the following morning did we know that Britain had been victorious in the Battle of Jutland, the largest naval encounter in history.

Jutland was no Trafalgar and heroic victory. Britain ended up losing more ships and men than the Germans – later discovered to be due to the type of explosive shells stored in our magazines that could detonate easily if the ship itself was hit. On the plus side, the British didn't fall for the German ruse of a retreat. If they had, they would have run into German mines. And the German Navy never really recovered. The Germans were technically superior but the British Navy could continue to blockade the German ports, causing untold misery to its civilians. I've been told that three quarters of a million civilians died in Germany of hunger and disease in the First World War. Many lived on just berries and potatoes. It was a major factor in the German government's decision to surrender.

I discovered later that John Travers Cornwell, who went to the same school as me, was awarded a Victoria Cross for bravery in the battle. He died in Grimsby Hospital on 2 June aged just 16. He was initially buried there, too, in a pauper's grave, but his body was later moved to Manor Park Cemetery in east London, where a memorial to him stands today. Cornwell was a messenger on HMS *Chester* who stayed at his post even though men were dying in droves around him. His father, a serving soldier, was later buried in the same grave.

It is a general assumption that the Battle of Jutland was the only naval battle of the Great War. There were in fact several major skirmishes, but this was the one and only occasion the British Grand Fleet fought the Imperial German Navy for total supremacy of the sea. It was fought on 31 May – 1 June 1916, in the North Sea near Jutland, the northward-pointing peninsular mainland of Denmark. The Imperial German Navy's High Seas Fleet was commanded by Vice-Admiral Reinhard Scheer whose intention was to lure out, trap and destroy a portion of the Grand Fleet, as he was mindful that his forces were insufficient in number to engage the entire British fleet at one time. This formed part of the overall German strategy of breaking the British naval blockade of the North Sea and allowing German mercantile shipping to operate again. The Royal Navy's British Grand Fleet – commanded by Admiral Sir John Jellicoe – on the other hand, was pursuing a strategy seeking to engage and destroy the High Seas Fleet or else keep the German force bottled up and away from Britain's own shipping lanes. Vital if Britain – as an island nation – was to keep its population fed, and its armed forces supplied on the continent.

The Germans' plan was to use Vice-Admiral Franz Hipper's fast scouting group of five modern battle cruisers to lure Vice-Admiral Sir David Beatty's battle cruiser squadrons through a submarine picket line and into the path of the main German fleet and so annihilate them. But the British had learned from signal intercepts that a major fleet operation was likely, and on 30 May Jellicoe sailed with the Grand Fleet to rendezvous with Beatty, passing the intended positions of the German submarine pickets before the submarines had reached those positions.

On the afternoon of 31 May Beatty encountered Hipper's battle cruiser force long before the Germans had expected, negating any submarine influence, but in a running battle Hipper successfully drew the British vanguard into the path of the High Seas Fleet. By the time Beatty turned towards the British main fleet he had lost two battle cruisers along with his numerical advantage over Hipper. However the German fleet in pursuit of Beatty to finish him off was drawn towards the main British fleet. As the sun was lowering on the western horizon backlighting the German forces, until nightfall two hours later the two huge fleets — totalling 250 ships between them — were heavily engaged firing thousands of shells.

Fourteen British and eleven German ships were sunk with great loss of life – 6,094 British seamen, and 2,551 German seafarers. After sunset, and throughout the night, Jellicoe desperately manœuvred to cut the Germans off from their base in hopes of joining battle in the morning, but under cover of darkness the Germans crossed the wake of the British fleet and returned to port.

Both sides would claim outright victory. The British had lost more ships and many more sailors – some high ranking such as Rear-Admiral Arbuthnot, whose flagship was spectacularly destroyed as its magazine was hit by a German salvo. This was a common problem amongst the British ships that had been destroyed and would be investigated by the Admiralty resulting in different shells being developed. The British press severely criticised the Grand Fleet's actions, but the German High Seas Fleet's plan of destroying Beatty's squadrons had also failed. The Germans continued to pose a threat that required the British to keep their battleships concentrated in the North Sea, but they never again contested control of the high seas. Instead, the German Navy turned its efforts and resources to unrestricted submarine warfare – ultimately highlighting to some that the days of the dreadnoughts ruling the waves had ended as a new technology took over.

After that I was posted to Bacton, north of Great Yarmouth, to take part in night-flying exercises. Here we slept under canvas. One of the biggest tasks was to make a flare path using petrol tins with their tops taken off. But night flying wasn't the only aerial challenge on the minds of fliers at the time.

One day Flight Sub Lieutenant T.G.C. Woods, better known as 'Little Woods' because of his small size, asked me if I could get him some stout cord before the afternoon's flying session. We got on well, despite the difference in rank. I had discovered a farm nearby, which I often visited. I went there to borrow ploughing rope hanging on the walls, choosing the lengths in best condition.

When I asked Woods how much rope he needed, he confided he was planning to loop the loop. This was frowned upon by commanders because of the threat to men and machines. However, that didn't worry me and I cut a length of some six yards and secured it around the cockpit seat of the BE2c so it would loop over both shoulders and was knotted at the back. Woods looked secure enough. With that I primed the prop, removed the chocks and held the tail, ready for take-off.

I watched with both fear and fascination as the plane climbed steeply. When it reached about 2,000 ft it appeared to hover for a moment and I thought he was going to do a tail slide, but he rocked a bit before diving off into a loop the loop. He did the same manoeuvre twice more before returning to the ground.

As soon as Woods landed I ran to the taxiing plane to cut him free. He was triumphant as we shook hands. Before the day was finished everyone knew of Woods' achievement. It was miraculous that he survived, really, given that the aircraft of the time were not built to withstand acrobatics.

The first man to try looping the loop is thought to be Frenchman Adolphe Pégoud, who performed the feat at Brooklands racecourse in Surrey in September 1913. He switched off the engine before turning the Blériot monoplane on its back. Afterwards, he said it was 'as comfortable as sitting at home in an armchair'. Pégoud later became the first ace to die in action.

In March 1917 two fliers were killed in a BE2c when they attempted a loop the loop. Flight Lieutenant E. Pulling and Sub Flight Lieutenant J. Northrop died after their BE2c broke up in mid-air during the manoeuvre.

When we were flying we couldn't stay airborne for long because we'd run out of fuel. That was the trouble. People sometimes had to ditch their aircraft. I saw several ditching, when the plane didn't have enough power. In about 12 months, that problem was overcome with better engines.

If I got a 48-hour pass then I would go and see Nanna and Uncle Charlie in London. I used to make an early start and caught the train, making my way to the dining car. While I was looking at the menu, the waiter would usually interrupt to say: 'The breakfast is on the gentleman over there.'

I would look over to the fellow and raise my hand. He would signal back. And it was always the same story on my return journey. I was always amazed and gratified at the kindness shown to me by complete strangers because I was in a uniform. Members of the public would treat me to a drink or a meal to say 'thank you' for helping to defend the country.

When war was declared there were street celebrations in most of Europe's capital cities, reflecting a conviction that a glorious outcome for the righteous was imminent. Within three months of the outbreak of war, however, there was stalemate throughout Europe and the forces of both sides dug in. That meant building a series of almost subterranean channels to shelter soldiers and equipment from enemy fire.

If the trench systems were intended to protect soldiers, then they failed as the British lacked the local materials as well as building techniques to match the German's for superior construction. Trenches and the men in them, became an irresistibly attractive target for ground bombardment and, increasingly, aerial attack. Living in cramped, unsanitary conditions, the soldiers in the trenches were exposed to numerous diseases.

Throughout the war, there were pushes and initiatives, defeats and retreats on both small and large scales along a front line that had various salients. Each Allied gain was inevitably followed by a German counter-attack that frequently snatched back the scraps of wasteland that had been taken. This is not the place for its detailed coverage. However, in brief, the longest battle of the war was Verdun, in which the German plan to 'bleed France white' went in fits and starts until it was finally abandoned after a year. Designed to be a hammer blow to France – and to accompany a submarine blockade of Britain that would starve it into submission – the Germans had one million troops to face just 200,000 defenders of the psychologically important forts in and around Verdun. There were notable German victories and appalling French casualties, and then the tide turned and France gained the upper hand. Eventually, little had been won or lost by the time the Germans pulled out of the vicinity, except for the lives of some million soldiers on both sides.

The Battle of the Somme was launched early, to help relieve pressure on the French at Verdun. One of the least productive campaigns ever conceived by the British military, it is remarkable mainly for the fact that over 19,000 British troops died on its opening day, 1 July 1916. In the same time frame, 6,000 Germans were killed or wounded. The Somme offensive was designed to wear down German resistance and make territorial gains. In fact, the plans were an ill-kept secret. And, after an eight-day (inaccurate) bombardment prior to the battle, the Germans were in no doubt about what was coming next. Unfortunately for the British, the bombardment failed to destroy enemy installations or barbed-wire defences. Hopes that soldiers would advance in organised formation through No Man's Land unopposed to gain the German front line were tragically misplaced. The French had better success but still won little in the land grab.

Despite the introduction of tanks by the British, the campaign was brought to a close in November, with little to show other than a mounting casualty list.

And yet, perhaps the most ill-fated battle was Gallipoli, the 1915 campaign by the Allies to capture Constantinople and open a sea route to Russia. Embedded Turkish troops under German command pinned down the invaders and rendered the attack a failure. By the start of 1916, the invasion of Gallipoli was called off in the wake of about 100,000 deaths. Politically, the two major casualties were Winston Churchill, who had backed the plans, and Kitchener.

On 6 June 1917 I celebrated my 21st birthday. I got the afternoon off to see Dorothy and she presented me with a birthday card. It was difficult to buy presents. Nobody had much money and there wasn't much in the shops. But I received 21 kisses from Dorothy by way of a present and that was enough for me.

At Great Yarmouth and Bacton we had plenty of time on our hands. When I didn't meet Dorothy I spent the evening studying or reading. I was doing another correspondence course, this time with the International Correspondence School in Kingsway, London. The course on workshop calculations cost me £6 and today I still have the books they sent.

One of the questions was this: 'Determine the number of cubic feet contained in a log with the bark on 20 ft long, the girth at one end being 70 inches and the other end being 60 inches.' Another was: 'Find the number of cubic feet in a square balk 18 ft long with a sectional area of 256 square inches one end and 144 square inches at the other end.' The answer to the first question is 31¼ cubic feet and to the second it is 25 cubic feet.

I did an arithmetic course as well, at a cost of £4. One of the questions was: 'If 0.17 of a quantity of oil amounts to 424.5 gallons, how many gallons are there in all?' The answer to that one is 2,497.06. Before you ask, no, I didn't remember the answers for 90 years. They were in the back of the book.

I have always read a lot of books and poetry in addition to the courses. When I meet children in schools I always tell them to read books to find out more. You can find a lot more in a book than you can find on the television.

A web of railway lines by now covered Europe and it was this that ensured men were mobilised by the millions. The proliferation of trains made a fundamental difference to the way war was conducted and there was a 'last man standing' feel to strategy and tactics. However, rail travel was not the only innovation in warfare. The newly invented car was clad in armour so that it could take its place at the front.

Of course, both trains and cars were easy targets, and rail tracks were soon destroyed by enemy firepower. Enter the tank, a First World War invention that in fact dated from previous centuries. The great innovator Leonardo da Vinci (1452–1519) drew up plans for an armoured vehicle that could be used to protect soldiers advancing on an enemy. Much later, at the start of the twentieth century, caterpillar tracks were created for agricultural purposes, although their potential for hauling guns was quickly spotted by the British military. Ultimately, Winston Churchill, as First Lord of the Admiralty, drew together the available technology to form 'landships' as a solution to the battlefield stalemate.

Although an object of derision when they first appeared on the Western Front, tanks finally proved their worth in the Battle of Cambrai in 1917, when they gained territory and prisoners in short order. Unfortunately, inexperienced infantrymen failed to capitalise on the machines' advantages, but the future of the tank emerged from that point.

While it was Britain that led the way in pioneering the use of tanks in warfare, when it came to submarines, the Germans were leagues ahead.

Their First World War campaign with submarines (called U-boats) got off to a faltering start. In the first month of the conflict, Germany lost four U-boats from its 20-strong fleet without sinking a ship. However, the U-boats' success was defined by their captains and there were some extraordinarily effective campaigners taking the helm.

The aim of the U-boats was to put Britain into a stranglehold by cutting off sea trade. In general, all warships were considered fair game, while merchant vessels were held up, their crews put into lifeboats and then the ship sunk. The most successful U-boat captain of the war fired only four torpedoes in his whole career, finishing off most of the trophy tonnage with his conning tower guns after the crew of the victim ship was made safe.

Not every captain abided by the rules, though, and the most infamous example of this is the sinking of the liner Lusitania *off the Irish coast in 1915. At least 1,500 people died including 128 Americans. This and similar attacks on other merchant vessels did much to modify opinion in America towards the British cause. At the time Americans were maintaining a neutral stance, but their response to the liner attack was so vociferous that the Germans reviewed their U-boat policy. Had the Germans continued, Britain might well have been starved into submission.*

Only when Britain introduced the convoy system in 1917, when ships travelled in large formations for protection, did the Allies negate the U-boat menace. After the war, when literally scores of U-boats had been made or were in production, the Allies divided up the fleet and stripped it of its technology.

Germany was also at the forefront of gas attacks. Although not the first to fire gas cylinders – the French made an initial foray into the arena without any success – the Germans made their use more effective. Before long, Britain was learning lessons from the enemy and replied in kind. The gases used in the First World War were tear gas, mustard gas, chlorine and phosgene. Their major drawback was that attackers were just as prone to the effects of the gas as the opposition, especially in windy conditions. As the distribution of gas became more effective, so did the defences against it. Rough sack hoods were eventually replaced with masks. While only a small percentage of First World War deaths were caused by gas, there were many casualties. In 1925 the use of gas in warfare was outlawed and remains so today.

seven

SERVICE ON THE WESTERN FRONT

HAVING SOLD MY MOTORBIKE on the runway at Great Yarmouth, I went to France in September 1917 to support the Royal Flying Corps and that's where I saw the soldiers from the trenches. My first sight of France was from the ferry boat. The port at Boulogne was crowded with soldiers like me. The first thing I did was to find myself a little café and buy some eggs and chips with French bread. With it I had some wine. Beer cost five pence but wine cost tuppence so I used to choose wine when most of the lads preferred beer. I had eggs and chips for lunch during a tour of the town and then had a third serving of eggs and chips before reporting back.

I got a night's flop there. It was the last time I slept in a bed for six months. I joined No. 12 Squadron RNAS at Petite-Synthe near Dunkirk, which was equipped with Sopwith Pups and Camels to fly over the Western Front.

The Sopwith Pup was developed in 1916, a small single-seater fighter aircraft that was ideal for aircraft carrier landings. On 2 August 1917 Edwin Dunning became the first man to land a plane on a moving ship, HMS *Furious*. The Sopwith Camel, perhaps the most successful plane of the war, entered service at Dunkirk in 1917. Another single seater, it was more unwieldy than the planes we'd begun with. Ironically, more men lost their lives learning how to fly it than died using it in combat.

In the air I was an observer, by now armed with a machine gun which was far better at protecting oneself from attack than a .303 Enfield. I also used to sit behind the pilot and drop bombs when required – there was no art to this, just plain luck. On the ground I was a mechanic responsible for maintenance of the machine and the gun, salvaging any parts we could from crashed planes as and when we could locate them. At that difficult time, my squadron was operational almost around the clock. For three and a half months, ground strafing and bombing continued day and night. Our aircraft had targets on the front line and more strategic ones further behind enemy lines. We had it to do and we just got on with it. I learned to hear all, see all and say nowt. We had a job to do, and did it, and it was concentrating on that that got us through the war.

What we went through was nothing compared to the boys on the front line in the trenches, and I used to see them coming off the line to rest and refit. They came out of the trenches like hermit crabs, weighed down with kit. It was these men in the trenches who won the war, in my view. Everybody did their bit but we couldn't all be in the trenches and they did very well. I think they were the ones that had the most hardship.

At Ypres, known to the British troops as Wipers, the men had to eat standing in the trenches, with water up to their knees. They got trench foot through that. They had to live there for two weeks, eat their food, sleep and other things. How they managed I don't know but they did.

Really and truly, you got so used to men dying that you never mentioned them again. All the time I was there I didn't get to know that many very well. I was a bit of a loner. And you don't know much about what's going on. You don't even know what happens down the road except by jungle drums. People think that because you were there you know all about it. You don't. You only know one little bit. The only blokes who knew everything were the ones who ran the war.

I saw a lot of war in a little time. It was just the luck of the game. I took it in my stride. I saw the Gurkhas in action. I didn't think it was legal, what they did to the enemy. They were brutally efficient in war, and quite rightly the Germans were terrified of them, they just didn't fear death. [During the First World War more than 100,000 Gurkhas fought in the battles of Loos, Givenchy, Neuve Chapelle and Ypres as well as in Mesopotamia.]

You can't be the fairy on the Christmas tree all the time. I got some good jobs and some bad ones. But that was war. You had a job to do and you got on with it, without question and to the best of your ability. With me I carried a Bible given to me by Dorothy; it was a translation of the Old and New Testaments. On the flyleaf she wrote: 'May the Lord watch between thee and me while we are absent from one another. With all my fondest love and very best wishes for your welfare. Dorothy.' The inscription was dated 19 September 1917. She placed pressed flowers between the pages, which, like me, have survived these 90 years.

The print is extremely small in this Bible. But my eyesight was very good then and I read it from cover to cover. The lads used to chaff me and pull my leg. They asked how far I had got, whether I'd reached the bit about forbidden fruit. But books, papers and written material were in extremely short supply and were treasured. They were read and re-read continuously during a lull in activity. We were starved of news while we were in France.

The Bible from Dorothy was a thoughtful gift. I had taken religious instruction while I was in Great Yarmouth and was confirmed in the parish church on 23 March 1917 at 7.30 p.m. by the Lord Bishop of Norwich, Dr B. Pollock and Rev. Chas Moore, RN.

Planes were becoming more reliable and had a longer range than ever before. In 1914 the commonly used BE2c plane had a top speed of 72 mph, had a 90 horsepower engine and stayed airborne for a maximum of three hours. Just three years later the SE5a flew at 97 mph, had a 200 horsepower engine and could stay operational for eight hours.

I can clearly remember that, for the first time, the British had superior aircraft in numbers and models to the Germans. But what I didn't know was that there were proposals to merge the Royal Flying Corps and the Royal Naval Air Services.

There were many factors that contributed to the eventual defeat of Germany and the Ypres offensive of 1917 was one of them. The British Army came out of the Third Battle of Ypres in relatively good order considering what happened; they had suffered but were battle hardened and with morale intact to a degree. I was part of the force moving forward on the Ypres salient. I remember coming back from the lines in a lorry with an infantryman next to me. He was scarred between his thumb and forefinger across his wrist and arm, I remarked how lucky he had been and asked how he was wounded. He told me he was a sniper, called in to a particular section of the line to deal with a troublesome German sharpshooter.

'I took up position and carefully scoured the ground in front of me through my rifle sights,' he explained. 'Suddenly I spotted him and fired. Almost immediately I felt a burning sensation as his bullet struck my hand and the butt of the rifle. We must have fired almost simultaneously. I was told later they did not have any more problems so I must have got him.'

During my first leave from France I was travelling by train to Great Yarmouth when a young woman carrying a baby got into the same compartment. She was helped by a porter who placed her bag in the luggage rack above. Immediately, she noticed my uniform. 'You're in the Royal Naval Air Service,' she declared. 'I wonder, did you know my husband?'

She was married to a pilot, she explained, called Lieutenant Edwards who had been killed in action in France. I realised she meant Bunny Edwards, who had been shot in the groin in flight. Although he managed to land the plane, he was bleeding so profusely that he quickly died. I was there when it happened and had cursed the fact that we were never taught how to deal with casualties.

I was startled and struggled for words. What could I say to this young mother who was clearly still grieving for her husband? Soon I composed myself and told her that, no, he didn't suffer. His death was thankfully quick and that he had been a great pilot.

As soon as the train drew in to the next station I got out of the carriage and went to find another. I could hardly believe the coincidence. And I didn't even know that Edwards was married, let alone a father. What a shocking situation to face. And I've wondered since, if I had known first aid and applied pressure to the wound, could I have saved his life? I've thought about that a lot over the years.

After I had been in France for a few months I was offered the chance to return to England for officer training. That was a great accolade as not many men from the ranks were commissioned. I explained I wanted to talk it over with Dorothy before accepting anything.

I slipped a 20-franc note into my papers hoping it would do the trick of getting me home quickly. It did the trick as when I got to the jetty a petty officer got me on to a destroyer leaving from Dunkirk almost immediately. Back home again in England I went straight to Great Yarmouth to surprise Dorothy. After she made me a cup of tea I told her that I had been offered a commission in the RNAS. Her aunt and uncle gave me warm congratulations but Dorothy was quiet.

Later, when we were alone, she asked: 'What happens when the war is over?' I thought I was saying the right thing when I told her I would have a job for life. But she burst into tears and told me she didn't want me to stay in the forces, that she couldn't bear the long separations and anxiety about not knowing if I would come home again.

'Don't worry, it's not like that,' I told her, certain I would not be killed like countless thousands of others. Then I heard myself saying, 'Well, will you marry me then?'

I still can't understand why I did it, I hadn't planned to. I've often thought about it. Maybe it was because Dorothy was so upset and frightened. I had never seen her like that before and I was at a loss for words to comfort her and allay her fears.

We hugged each other and, through her tears, she said, 'Yes.' We were going to get married straight away, before I returned to France. But it was just not possible, although everyone was delighted with the announcement. In the end I applied for leave to be married after I returned to France. We were married on 21 March 1918 at St Chad's, the parish church in Chadwell Heath, Essex. I wore my uniform while Dorothy was in a day dress and carried a posy of spring flowers. Nanna Foster and Auntie Rosie were the witnesses. After a celebration drink we made our way to the railway station to catch a train to Maldon in Essex. There we booked a room in the White Swan for three nights. There was a war on. We had little time and not much money. But we promised each other that, if we were blessed with children, we would make sure they had the best wedding possible. I returned to my unit, a married man, while Dorothy went to live with Auntie Rosie and Uncle Charlie.

After the US joined the war in 1917, the Americans who had trained with us wanted to leave to be with their own people, naturally.

Henry returned to the front line midway through the Third Battle of Ypres, also known as Passchendaele. It began almost exactly a year after the wasteful Somme offensive, with hauntingly similar outcomes in terms of losses compared to ground gained. Once again, the Allied bombardment alerted the Germans of impending attack. Hopes that the progressive attrition of the Germans would result in their capitulation were not fulfilled. This time, unseasonal weather dogged Allied soldiers as they tried vainly to push ahead. With August came heavy rainfall that, together with the shelling, turned the landscape into a boggy moonscape without trees or buildings, grass or bushes. At the best of times this was marshy land. Now this was the worst of times, after the drainage systems were destroyed in the initial bombardment. Soldiers drowned in enveloping mud, weighed down by greatcoats and packs made lead-heavy by rainfall. With only three dry days in August 1917 it became increasingly difficult to move around. Soldiers depended on duckboards, wooden pathways across the muddy terrain, for survival.

Tanks proved useless while the German machine-gunners sheltered in thick concrete bunkers, christened 'pillboxes' by the Allies. The Allies did have air superiority, though, which is where Henry's squadron would have had to work round the clock to maintain. However, the Germans had been ordered not to surrender Passchendaele under any circumstances. Every assault met determined resistance and, in one battle, 1,000 yards was won for the cost of 1,321 lives.

Still British and French generals would not backtrack. Field Marshal Douglas Haig (1861–1928), a cavalryman, continued to expect horses to win the day, regardless of the changing face of war. Despite the climbing body count among British, French, Australian and South African soldiers and the patent lack of success of the offensive, Haig refused to call off the attack. Instead, he chose the Canadians for the final push. Their commander, Arthur Currie, gloomily predicted victory would cost at least 16,000 Canadian lives.

In November 1917, with a total gain of five miles in four months of fighting, the Canadians took over the crumbled, smoking wreckage that was Passchendaele. Currie was unnervingly accurate. Of the 260,000 Allied casualties, a shade under 16,000 were Canadians. Only months later the village was surrendered without a fight during the 1918 spring offensive by Germany. Later, Winston Churchill called it 'a forlorn expenditure of valour and life without equal in futility'.

The Third Battle of Ypres (or Passchendaele) was the final enactment of the 'one more push' grand strategy, that the stalemate of trench warfare could be broken by brute offensive action against fixed positions. The massive and tactically meaningless casualty levels – coupled with the horrendous conditions in which the battle was fought – damaged Field Marshal Haig's reputation and made the Third Ypres emblematic of the horror of industrialised attritional warfare.

I remember getting my wound. It happened when I was at St Pol aircraft depot. We were shelled by a large gun, a Leugenboom. This gun fired 15-inch shells at the rate of one every eight minutes. The range must have been 27 miles or so across German-held territory, right on target. It coincided with a three-pronged air attack and also shells from German ships. I was later told after the war that it had been the very first recorded three-pronged air attack in aviation history – not that I would have been happy at that fact!

We were certainly caught with our pants down and the depot took a pasting. There was nowhere to find cover so we ended up lying in a crater. Suddenly I felt a burning sensation in my arm and saw that a sliver of shrapnel had grazed me. There's not much of a scar now. It wasn't all that bad.

As Henry testifies, the life of aircrews on the Western Front was anything but easy or safe for that matter. Even though based behind the front line, both sides targeted one another's airfields as key areas to be destroyed. In the air, over enemy territory, pilots obviously had to contend with batteries of search lights, machine-gun fire and rockets from the German lines. But, behind the lines – such as where Henry was serving – the air bases were constantly attacked as they became a focus for German bombing, as the following account from rafinfo. org.uk, an internet history site, reveals.

On 31 July 1917, the Battle of Ypres commenced and from then until mid-November, when the battle ended, the Allies waged a vigorous and unremitting air offensive in support of the Army. The RNAS squadrons . . . kept up constant day and night attacks on enemy airfields and coastal targets. They also bombed railway stations, junctions and depots in an attempt to isolate the battlefield. This was one of the earliest examples of the use of aircraft in the interdiction role. On the night of 16 August, Nos. 7 and 7a Squadrons made their most successful night attack. In support of the British Army's attack at Lanemarck, they raided the Thourout railway junction and ammunition dumps with 14 aircraft, all of which found and bombed the target.

Nine tons of bombs were dropped, ranging from 65 to 250 pounds. Explosions were still taking place 90 minutes after the last aircraft left the target area and the fires were visible from behind the British trenches.

During this autumn of 1917, the Flanders RNAS Command reached the peak of its bombing power. Attacks such as the one on Thourout became commonplace and the tonnage of bombs increased to an average of 6 tons per raid during September. Between the nights of 2 and 4 September, Nos. 7 and 7a Squadrons dropped over 16 tons of bombs on the Bruges docks alone. The amount of destruction achieved by these raids is perhaps best shown by the importance attached by the German High Command to the elimination of the Dunkirk Command.

From September, the towns and airfields of the Dunkirk Command were subjected to nightly attacks from land, sea and air. So intense were these attacks that the RNAS Aircraft Depot was forced to decentralise into a series of sub-depots and parks. Severe though these raids were, they completely failed in their main aim of curtailing Allied bombing. Not only did Allied bombing increase but the scope of targets was widened.

I had other assignments, too. Once I was travelling around the countryside in a Crossley tender with a surveyor. Our task was to survey sites for proposed airfields. My job was to hold the theodolite as he charted the measurements. It was a good number.

Fortunately, I usually moved across battle areas in transport, unlike the infantry. The infantry was regularly rotated from the firing line to the support and reserve lines and then back to billets located well behind the firing line. Invariably, all such repositioning was done on foot. The Slade Wallace equipment, dating from 1888, was used during the Boer War and again in the First World War. Canvas webbing was tailored and designed to distribute about 60 lb of equipment weight evenly over the body. The webbing held 150 rounds of ammunition, a bayonet, an entrenching tool, water bottle, rations, gas mask and spare clothing together with the soldier's .303 rifle. Infantrymen were paid a shilling a day, which increased to a shilling and sixpence in 1917.

When they weren't fighting, the men in the trenches had to carry out repairs and dig sleeping bays in the bottom of the trench wall. Most of the work was done during the hours of darkness. Our trenches were nothing like as good as the German ones, and many times I heard Tommies on leave tell stories of the hell they had to endure there – frostbite and trench foot in the winter; flies and baking heat in the summer – and lice, always lice!

On the Western Front, the small improvised trenches of the first few months rapidly grew deeper and more complex, gradually becoming vast areas of interlocking defensive works. Such defensive works resisted both artillery barrages and mass infantry assaults. The space between the opposing trenches was referred to as 'No Man's Land' (for its lethal uncrossability) and varied in width depending on the battlefield. On the Western Front it was typically between 100 and 300 yards (90-275 m), though only 30 yards (27 m) on Vimy Ridge. After the German withdrawal to the Hindenburg line in March 1917, it stretched to over a kilometre in places.

So, the scene was now set for the opposing blocs of armies to attack and counter-attack across 'No Man's Land' over the next four years, seeking the breakthrough to the green fields beyond that would ultimately yield to victory. This doctrine was not only a failure of outdated tactics against modern weaponry, but would lead to unimaginable loss of life, such as on the first day of the Battle of the Somme – the British Army's singular heaviest defeat in history when over 60,000 men were either killed or wounded.

The Germans made something of a science out of designing and constructing defensive works. They used reinforced concrete to construct deep, shell-proof, ventilated dugouts, as well as strategic strong points. They were more willing than their opponents to make a strategic withdrawal to a superior prepared defensive position. When British troops captured enemy trench systems, they would often celebrate at their good fortune in now having proved defensive lines that would protect them far better than their own. The Germans were also the first to apply the concept of 'defence in depth', where the front-line zone was hundreds of yards deep and contained a series of redoubts rather than a continuous trench. Each redoubt could provide supporting fire to its neighbours, and while the attackers had freedom of movement between the redoubts, they would be subjected to withering enfilade fire. The British eventually adopted a similar approach, but it was incompletely implemented when the Germans launched the 1918 "Spring Offensive" and proved disastrously ineffective.

I was never in the front line but I still experienced disturbed and troubled sleep. For a start, we slept where we could, often under a lorry, for example. It was a case of dropping down on the ground with a blanket. And, as I listened to the guns pounding, I couldn't help but think that a dawn attack was imminent and that young men like myself would soon be dead from bullets and shells. After the war I suffered with nightmares.

An individual infantry soldier's time in the front-line trench was usually brief; from as little as one day to as much as two weeks at a time before being relieved. A typical British soldier's year could be divided as follows:

15 per cent front line; 10 per cent support line; 30 per cent reserve line; 20 per cent rest; 25 per cent other (hospital, travelling, leave, training courses, etc.)

Even when in the front line, the soldier typically would only be called upon to engage in fighting a handful of times a year – making an attack, defending against an attack or participating in a raid. The frequency of combat would increase for the men of the 'elite' fighting divisions – on the Allied side: the British regular divisions, the Canadian Corps, the French XX Corps and the Anzacs.

Some sectors of the front saw little activity throughout the war, making life in the trenches comparatively easy, while other sectors were in a perpetual state of war. On the Western Front, Ypres – where Henry served – was invariably hellish, especially for the British in the exposed, overlooked salient. However, quiet sectors still amassed daily casualties through sniper fire, artillery, disease and poison gas. In the first six months of 1916, before the launch of the disastrous Somme Offensive, the British did not engage in any significant battles on their sector of the Western Front and yet suffered 107,776 casualties. About one in eight men would return alive and wound-free from the trenches.

There were food and supplies dumps behind the line that were not for storing explosives. That was the same for both sides and there was an unwritten agreement that they were never bombed. One day the Germans broke the code and shelled our dumps. They suffered a terrible retribution as we shelled their dumps for a week. It never occurred again.

Airfields could only be created with the use of transport. As many as 50 lorries at one time carried the essentials, such as aircraft spares, fuel, oil and so forth. Often lorries would get bogged down on marshy terrain or slither into shell holes. We used to have to drag them out. We carried chains specifically for that, and it was a long, hard job. Chinese labourers assisted with the loading, unloading and erecting of the gear. I've no idea how they got involved. I can remember one tragic incident when a group of Chinese workers huddled together to look at a hand grenade that one had found. Inevitably the pin became dislodged, killing all of them.

During the great German offensive launched by Ludendorff in March of 1918, my squadron was retreating just like everyone else. The Germans had a new way of breaking down our defences with their highly trained stormtrooper units who wreaked havoc on the front lines, gaining ground unheard of before. It was a close run thing but the Allies managed to hold them and slowly push them back by the end of the summer. That was a busy time for us all.

The RNAS only brought up things for aircraft. There was very little spare clothing – or even food. My boots had deteriorated so much that they were letting in water and feeling really uncomfortable. But there was nothing the RNAS could do for me, so I went to the Army and asked at the quartermaster's stores. The only boots they had were of the hobnail variety, which were not suitable for clambering over aircraft. But the man there sent me to the depot down the road where there was a lot of surplus. 'They might be able to help you,' he said.

It was a depot run by the War Graves Commission people. I explained what I was looking for and one of the men there said a body had just arrived; perhaps his boots would fit.

I could see a pair of leather boots sticking over the end of the stretcher. 'If you want those, you can have them,' said the fellow. 'He won't have use for them any more.'

I was a bit taken aback and asked if I had to take them off. I asked whether men were normally buried with their boots on. Some were, some weren't, came the reply. The aim was to get the

dead bodies in the ground as soon as possible. This one was due
to go in an unmarked grave because no one knew his name, I was
told. I think he was a French soldier. After thinking about it for a
few moments, I took the boots and put them to good use.

*On 1 April 1918 the RNAS, with its 67,000 personnel and nearly
3,000 aircraft, was merged with the Royal Flying Corps and the Royal
Air Force was created. The merger seems to have been the product
of a Parliamentary debate and inquiry in 1917 to discuss the effect
air power could have on industrial nations in wartime. It had been
assumed a new air service would be created to balance the already
existing RNAS and RFC. However, under a new Air Ministry, it
was decided to amalgamate the two wings into one general purpose
formation, so eliminating any rivalries that existed between the air
wings of the Army and Navy which was seen as divisive. Now the
general idea was to throw everything against Germany in an aerial
hammer blow, introducing strategic bombing for the first time.*

Even after the Royal Air Force was formed, I still considered myself
a Royal Navy man. It wasn't until much later that I realised what
a momentous event had taken place and that I was at the heart of
it. When I sit here and discuss it with Dennis it is a shock – as well
as a privilege – to think that I am the only man left alive from that
original reorganisation when the RAF was formed.

In the late spring of 1918 I met a group of artillerymen talking
about the war. They were at pains to tell me how many hundreds
and hundreds of Germans their guns had killed in the last month
during the failed German offensive. They painted a vivid picture
of Germans climbing over their dead to get to the front line. I
think they said that because there had been a lot of criticism of
the artillery in the early part of the war. Artillery bombardments
were supposed to clear the path ahead of barbed wire and German

emplacements and they just didn't. This time the artillerymen were fighting at point-blank range.

As 1918 wore on I found myself a few miles outside Poperinge in Belgium with some time on my hands. I had heard about a Salvation Army centre there and decided to drop in. When I got there the centre was full of about 400 khaki-clad troops. On an improvised stage at the end of the room there were men in soldiers' uniforms of a different kind, belonging to the Salvation Army.

The room was full of tobacco smoke, the hum of conversation and roars of laughter. It was subdued by the voice of a Salvation Army man. He apologised for the delay and explained that the pianist had not turned up. Was there a volunteer in the crowd who could play the piano? A few men were prodded by their mates but no one stepped forward. There was another urgent request and this time the Salvation Army man jumped from the stage to make his way through the crowd of men. And then there was another request – and another.

Reluctantly, I made my way forward, towards the piano. Grateful hands hauled me up on the stage. The service leader joined me and said, 'Now we can begin.' His words were greeted by loud claps, stomps and cheers. The first number, of course, was 'Onward Christian Soldiers'. Fortunately I remembered the opening chords and managed to accompany most of the hymns that day. I really enjoyed being a 'concert pianist' for the afternoon in front of such an appreciative audience. I made a promise that, if I survived the war, I would start piano lessons once more.

While I was in Poperinge I also visited Toc H, the rambling house rented to the British Army and run as a church and social club. Its strange name came from the army signaller's jargon for Talbot House, its full title. The first person I saw was Rev. Tubby Clayton (1885–1972) arranging a bowl of roses. Rev. Clayton beckoned me over to admire the flowers, newly arrived from Britain. The sight of them made me quite emotional. Rev. Clayton could see I was moved.

'Is this your first visit to Toc H?' he asked.

I said it was and he told me he was about to hold a communion service for a group of lads already there and invited me to join them. This was the first communion I had received since my days in Great Yarmouth. I met some really interesting people there, too, such as Louis Freeman, who was a professional violinist. He introduced me to Alfred Corto, the composer and concert pianist. Corto had been wounded in the heel of his foot and was transferred to the company guarding the airstrip at Dunkirk.

When the war ended on 11 November 1918 I was in Belgium. Everyone else wanted to have a party but I just wanted some undisturbed sleep. It was brilliant to get my head down. Outside they fired off every round of ammo they could get their hands on. I had had enough of fireworks. I had a really good night's rest instead.

Against the unlikely backdrop of sordid war, some fine poetry was produced that reflected both the aspirations and the abuses of the troops in the trenches. The tenor of the poems reflected both loyal and insubordinate attitudes among those charged with fighting the cause. Among the best remembered is Rupert Brooke (1887–1915), who died because a relatively minor injury was left untreated. He wrote when there was still a vestige of faith in the British cause, and was interpreted as one who glorified the war. He is best known for his oft-quoted words from 'The Soldier':

If I should die, think only this of me
That there's some corner of a foreign field
That is forever England.

Another poet, who died in the same year, adopted an altogether tougher line about the predicament of British soldiers. Dismissively, Charles Sorley (1895–1915) wrote: 'The voice of our poets and men of letters is finely trained and sweet to hear; it teems with sharp saws and rich sentiment: it is a marvel of delicate technique: it pleases, it flatters, it charms, it soothes: it is a living lie.' Sorley, a captain who died after being shot in the head by a sniper, was thought by some to be the literary world's greatest loss claimed by the war.

Perhaps the most famous of the war poets is Wilfred Owen (1893– 1918), who wrote some of the most pointed and provocative verses of the conflict. In his poem 'Anthem for Doomed Youth', he began with the line: 'What passing-bells for these who die as cattle?' Born in Oswestry, Shropshire, Owen didn't volunteer until halfway through the war. Letters to his mother, Susan, reveal something of his experiences. One reads:

> We eat & drink out of old tins, some of which show traces of ancient enamel. We are never dry, and never 'off duty' . . . On all the officers' faces there is a harassed look that I have never seen before, and which in England, never will be seen – out of jails . . . I censored hundreds of letters yesterday, and the hope of peace was in every one. . . . I am perfectly well and strong, but unthinkably dirty and squalid. I scarcely dare to wash. Pass on as much of this happy news as may interest people. The favourite song of the men is 'The Roses round the door/Makes me love Mother more.' They sing this everlastingly. I don't disagree.

Another letter related a slice of action Owen had seen:

> Twice in one day we went over the top, gaining both our objectives. Our A Company led the Attack, and of course

116

lost a certain number of men. I had some extraordinary escapes from shells & bullets. Fortunately there was no bayonet work, since the Hun ran before we got up to his trench . . . Never before has the Battalion encountered such intense shelling as rained on us as we advanced in the open. The Colonel sent round this message the next day: 'I was filled with admiration at the conduct of the Battalion under the heavy shellfire . . . The leadership of officers was excellent, and the conduct of the men beyond praise.' The reward we got for all this was to remain in the Line 12 days. For 12 days I did not wash my face, nor take off my boots, nor sleep a deep sleep. For 12 days we lay in holes, where at any moment a shell might put us out. I think the worst incident was one wet night when we lay up against a railway embankment. A big shell lit on the top of the bank, just two yards from my head. Before I awoke, I was blown in the air right away from the bank!

Owen died just seven days before the armistice. As the bells rang out to mark the war's conclusion on 11 November, his parents were being told of his death at their home in Shrewsbury.

When we moved we put all our gear on lorries, which was slow going. The Germans were very good at laying booby traps – ingenious and deadly contraptions that slowed our advance and helped the Germans to take their time during a retreat.

We could not move forward until we had cleared the traps. A group of Canadian engineers was with us to do that job but they hadn't had time to clear the area we found ourselves in one night, and they told us so. We were told to stay just where we were, to sleep on the ground where we stood.

I took off my boots and made my bed with a groundsheet and a blanket, quite used to this by now, and went to sleep immediately. But in the night I awoke and set off to answer a call of nature. I was disorientated, half asleep I suppose, and it was pitch black.

I took two or three steps forward and suddenly my legs gave way and I slid into mud and water up to my armpits. There were sudden movements around me and squealing, coming from the rats. And the smell was so foul. As far as I could see, there were dead rats, dead cats, dead mice and human flesh in the water. It was green muck and I was sinking into it!

Of course I had to get out. If I had moved to the right I would have fallen off the shelf of the shell hole and I wouldn't be here now to tell you. And, even though I went to the left, I never thought I was going to get out of that shell hole alive.

I inched along trying to find purchase for my feet. At the same time I could feel many inert objects floating against me. The darkness was intense. My feet sank either into mud or some unknown thing. What would people say, I thought, about the sailor who drowned on dry land? Finally I located some firm ground and hauled my body onto the shore. With my heart pounding I lay there, gasping for breath. I knew I had to stay where I was until daylight. I wasn't going to take another risk that night.

At dawn I got back to my bed and lay down – still shaking. The shell hole had been created by our own guns and was strewn with barbed wire entanglements. I was lucky to get out alive. My uniform had dried on my body. We all got lice in our clothes, even without dips in shell holes. We used to run the seam of the shirt over a candle flame to get rid of them. It wasn't until I got into Germany, when I was billeted with a German family, that the uniform was cleaned properly and I felt human again.

The woman who lived there gave me a blanket one night and she cleaned every rag on my back. From what I understood she bashed it against a stone to get the filth out of the material. It was all fresh and dry for me the following morning. To thank her I went to the quartermaster's store, but all I managed to get was two bars of Sunlight soap, which I gave to her. It was all I could get to repay her kindness but she cherished them.

By the time we got to Germany, people were starving. Workers in the munitions factories who had protested during the war were now going on strike because of food shortages. When I encountered ersatz bread for the first time it had a profound and terrible effect on my digestive system. It was more like coal than bread and it gave me the worst indigestion I had ever suffered. The people in Germany didn't want war any more than we did. We did all we could for them. They did all they could for us. In Germany they couldn't do enough for you.

By the end of the war, in 1918, the casualty figures were immense. Given the different arenas of war and the effect of disease, it is difficult to state figures with any accuracy, but all the major players were mourning huge losses. Despite its withdrawal from the conflict in 1917, Russia suffered the most. This was because its soldiers were generally ill-trained and badly equipped and its commanders inept. The death toll of Russians was in the region of 1,700,000. The British death tally of about 910,000 was less than that of the French, who lost 1,357,800. In Germany there were 1,774,000 war dead and in Austro-Hungary 1,200,000. Worldwide, the First World War death toll stood at more than 8.5 million, alongside a casualty figure of more than 37.5 million.

On the flip side of this coin are the countries who joined the war but suffered fewer consequences of it. Indeed, some countries only put their name to a declaration when the conflict was nearly over, in the hope of getting some of the spoils of a peace settlement. Countries involved in the First World War – listed as they were known in that era – include Albania, Arabia, Brazil, China, Costa Rica, Cuba,

Finland, Greece, Guatemala, Haiti, Honduras, Japan, Liberia, Luxembourg, Montenegro, Nicaragua, Panama, Persia, Philippines, Poland, Portugal and colonies, San Marino and Siam.

At Christmas 1918, shortly after the end of the war, I was billeted with a German family on the Rhine bank. I can't remember the name of the family but I believe the father was a jeweller by trade. On Christmas Eve I was invited into the study to celebrate the season. I was pretty good at French and the jeweller's son also spoke it, so that's how we communicated.

The jeweller stood at his desk and dispensed Christmas parcels to the staff. Then came a knock at the door. The jeweller's wife entered cautiously. She spoke to him and he offhandedly barked his reply. Immediately she left. I got to the door just in time to open it for her.

But the next day the jeweller presented her with some glittering items and she wrapped herself around him and kissed him. What a difference a day made. The children wished me a Happy Christmas on behalf of the family. I was touched by their affectionate display.

Although I didn't have gifts for them I did have two Jaffa oranges sent to me by Dorothy. I have no idea how she got hold of them. I went upstairs and presented them to the children. Their eyes lit up and they ran off, delighted, to show their parents. I often wonder whether they are still alive today.

After that I was posted to Cologne. We stopped in a Cologne hotel that had a chef who had once worked in London for ten or twelve years. Cologne cathedral was beautiful, it really was. We had a lovely room opposite there.

The water in a park lake was frozen while I was there and children used it for skating. One day, as I walked in the park, I heard screams after one boy crashed through the ice and disappeared. I rushed over and managed to fish him out. His mother was overjoyed and took me back to her home. Although we didn't speak the same language I understood she wanted me to accept something from a drawer of knives by way of a thank you. I accepted two, made my excuses and left.

There was hardly anything to do while we were at the aerodrome at Bumonoet, outside Cologne. We just had to sit out the time and wait to be demobbed. We were glad to get home.

While I was stationed in Germany, I cannot recall exactly where I was at that time, I was disciplined and put on a charge. It all started with an innocent prank – I had been larking around with some naval ratings, just to pass the time. Their chief petty officer came along and bawled his men out, but he couldn't really say much to me. In the RNAS we were seen as being in a privileged position. But suddenly he put me on a charge, apparently for 'exciting hilarity'. I had to report to an officer in charge the following morning at 9 a.m. When I came to report to the defaulters parade, the charge had changed to 'keeping a dirty tent'. When I analysed what had gone on, I reckoned the chief petty officer was simply jealous of me because, like other RNAS servicemen, I had a tent of my own while he had to share with others. I had to plead guilty to the charge. There was nothing else to be said. But when I went back later to explain myself, the commanding officer said, 'Don't worry about it.' He explained the punishment was to spend the next few days working for his department. There were many worse punishments than this so I didn't say another word. I'm pleased to say the charge never appeared in my records.

During that time, a young rating called Johnston – the OC's driver – sought me out to inform me I had to help him on convoy, which was mainly supplying water to the camp. To my surprise the OC joined us too. When we got to the supply depot the OC looked out for the convoy saying we'd be back in an hour – the work wasn't actually that taxing; indeed after the fighting it was easy really. In the end, for the rest of that week, I took over the driving, helping the OC arrange billets for the RNAS staff as our number increased. One particular day, though, Johnston was driving the Crossley and we encountered a lot of activity on the road – British Military Police, or Red Caps, were everywhere. The OC told me to pull over and went to find out what was going on. We were informed that Lord Haig was setting up his HQ in the town we were thinking of going to ourselves. On hearing the news, our OC turned and shouted, 'Johnston, drive like hell away from here!'

Recently I've seen my records for the first time. They tell me that I joined the RNAS on 21 September 1915, aged nineteen and three months. I was 5 ft 6 in. tall, with a 35-in. chest, light brown hair, blue eyes and a fair complexion. I had hammer toes on both feet and a scar on my right arm. Initially I was a second-class air mechanic. On 15 December 1916 I was acting air mechanic and four months later I was acting mechanic first class. I was transferred to the RAF with the number RAF 208317.

I'm extremely proud of the achievements made by the RNAS in the First World War – we certainly made an impact both at sea and of course on the Western Front. Without those early days and our scrappy little biplanes, the First World War couldn't have been won. It was wonderful to have been part of it and I'll never forget the men whom I served with and those that died in action.

Today the focus of Armistice Day remains the Cenotaph in London, where royalty and dignitaries tend to mark the solemn occasion, as well as local war memorials. Initially made from wood and plaster, the Cenotaph was designed by Sir Edward Lutyens (1869–1944) at the request of Prime Minister Lloyd George. Its name is Greek for 'empty tomb'. Devoid of religious symbolism and adorned with only a simple inscription, 'The Glorious Dead', the Cenotaph's almost austere appearance proved popular and by the following year it had been reproduced in Portland stone.

The Cenotaph was unveiled on the same day as the funeral of the 'Unknown Warrior', an unidentified British soldier killed on a European battlefield during the First World War. He was buried in Westminster Abbey, London on 11 November 1920, the earliest such tomb honouring the unknown dead of the First World War.

THE UNKNOWN WARRIOR

The idea of a tomb of the Unknown Warrior was first conceived in 1916 by the Rev. David Railton, who while serving as an army chaplain on the Western Front, had seen a grave marked by a rough cross, which bore the pencil-written legend 'An Unknown British Soldier'. In 1920 he corresponded with the Dean of Westminster proposing that an unidentified British soldier from the battlefields in France be buried with due ceremony in Westminster Abbey 'amongst the kings' to represent the many hundreds of thousands who had died serving the British Empire. The idea was endorsed by the Dean and the then Prime Minister Lloyd George. There was initial opposition from King George V (who feared it might reopen the wounds of all the losses suffered by Britain in the Great War) and others but a outpouring of emotional support from the great number of bereaved families ensured its adoption and implementation.

Arrangements were placed in the hands of Lord Curzon of Kedleston who prepared in committee the service and location. The body was chosen from four bodies draped with Union Jacks at the chapel at St Pol near Arras, France on the night of 7 November 1920 by Brigadier General L.J. Wyatt and Lieutenant Colonel E.A.S. Gell. The remains were placed in a simple pine coffin. The coffin stayed at the chapel overnight and on the afternoon of 8 November, *it was transferred under guard to the castle library within the citadel at Boulogne. Troops lined the route and a company from the French 8th Infantry regiment, recently awarded the Légion d'Honneur en masse, stood vigil over it overnight. The following morning, the coffin was transferred into a casket of the oak timbers of trees chosen from Hampton Court Palace. The casket was banded with iron and a medieval crusader's sword, chosen by George V personally from the Royal Collection, was affixed to the top and surmounted by an iron shield bearing the inscription 'A British Warrior who fell in the Great War 1914–1918 for King and Country'.*

The casket was then placed on a military wagon, drawn by six black horses. At 10.30 a.m., all church bells of Boulogne tolled; the massed trumpets of French cavalry and bugles of French infantry played the Aux Champs – the French 'Last Post'. Then, the mile-long procession – led by 1,000 French schoolchildren and with a division of French soldiers forming the guard of honour – made its way down to the harbour. At the quayside, Marshal Foch saluted the casket before it was carried up the gangway of the destroyer, HMS Verdun, and piped aboard with an admiral's call. The Verdun slipped anchor just before noon and was joined by an escort of six battleships. As the flotilla carrying the casket closed on Dover Castle it received a 19-gun Field Marshal's salute. It was landed at Dover Maritime Railway Station at the Western Docks on 10 November, from where it was taken to Victoria Station, where it arrived at platform 8 at 8.32 p.m. that evening and remained for the night of the 10th – at both locations there is a plaque. Every year on 11 November there is a small Remembrance service at Victoria Station between platforms 8 and 9.

On the morning of 11 November 1920 the casket was loaded onto a gun carriage of the Royal Horse Artillery and drawn by six horses through immense and silent crowds. The route followed was Hyde Park Corner, The Mall and to Whitehall, where the Cenotaph was unveiled by King George V. The cortège was then followed by the King, Royal Family and ministers of state to Westminster Abbey, where the casket was borne into the West Nave of the Abbey flanked by a guard of honour of 100 recipients of the Victoria Cross.

The guests of honour were a group of about 100 women. They had been chosen because each had lost her husband and all her sons in the war. The coffin was then interred in the far western end of the nave, only a few feet from the entrance, with soil from each of the main battlefields, and covered with a silk pall. The armed services then stood as honour guard as tens of thousands of mourners filed past. The ceremony appears to have served as a form of catharsis for collective mourning on a scale not previously known.

The grave was then capped with a black Belgian marble stone (the only tombstone in the Abbey on which it is forbidden to walk) featuring this inscription, composed by Dean Ryle, Dean of Westminster, engraved with brass from melted down wartime ammunition:

BENEATH THIS STONE RESTS THE BODY OF A BRITISH WARRIOR
UNKNOWN BY NAME OR RANK BROUGHT FROM FRANCE TO LIE
AMONG THE MOST ILLUSTRIOUS OF THE LAND AND BURIED HERE
ON ARMISTICE DAY 11 NOV: 1920, IN THE PRESENCE OF HIS
MAJESTY KING GEORGE V HIS MINISTERS OF STATE THE CHIEFS
OF HIS FORCES AND A VAST CONCOURSE OF THE NATION

THUS ARE COMMEMORATED THE MANY MULTITUDES WHO
DURING THE GREAT WAR OF 1914 - 1918 GAVE THE MOST
THAT MAN CAN GIVE LIFE ITSELF FOR GOD FOR KING AND
COUNTRY FOR LOVED ONES HOME AND EMPIRE FOR THE
SACRED CAUSE OF JUSTICE AND THE FREEDOM OF THE WORLD

THEY BURIED HIM AMONG THE KINGS BECAUSE HE HAD
DONE GOOD TOWARD GOD AND TOWARD HIS HOUSE

Around the main inscription are four texts:

[TOP]   THE LORD KNOWETH THEM THAT ARE HIS

[SIDE]   UNKNOWN AND YET WELL KNOWN, DYING AND
         BEHOLD WE LIVE

[SIDE]   GREATER LOVE HATH NO MAN THAN THIS

[BASE]   IN CHRIST SHALL ALL BE MADE ALIVE

In addition to the Cenotaph there was a tremendous growth of war memorials of different shapes and sizes across the whole country. The war had claimed numerous lives and soon afterwards the government conceded it could not bring back all the bodies of the dead. Many families touched by war had no grave to visit and no place in which to contemplate their loss. The communities of villages, towns and cities likewise sought a place to mark their collective grief, through which they also wanted to express their national and personal pride. Thus war memorials were community initiatives paid for by local people and sponsored by councils. Most of the country's 37,000 war memorials were put in place between 1919 and 1922. Not everywhere had a memorial in mind; there were 'thankful' villages, so-called because all the local men and women who went to war returned home. Henry recalls that there were at least five of these villages at the time that probably are still listed today.

Remembrance services are marked by a two-minute silence – which still holds sway today. This was originally the idea of Australian journalist Edward George Honey, who published his thoughts in the London Evening News *in the spring of 1919. The notion was drawn to the attention of King George V, who instituted the silence as a way of softening the rawness of the first Armistice Day: 'All locomotion should cease so that, in perfect stillness, the thoughts of everyone may be concentrated on reverent remembrance of the glorious dead.' For years everything fell into a respectful hush on the closest Sunday to Armistice Day. Traffic – albeit lighter than today – came to a halt and pedestrians would stop in their tracks, heads bowed, as a mark of respect.*

Soon afterwards, poppies were distributed as a token of remembrance. A species native to northern Europe, poppies are abundant when the soil they seed in is disturbed. Consequently, soldiers serving in the trenches of the Western Front were often struck by the sight of the blood-red flowers sprouting in the carnage all around them. The poppies are mentioned in the popular poem by Canadian surgeon John McCrae – 'In Flanders Fields'. Lieutenant Colonel McCrae was serving with the Canadian Army as a doctor on the Western Front, and treated casualties at the Second Battle of Ypres in 1915. His friend – Lieutenant Alexis Helmer – was killed in the battle and his subsequent burial inspired McCrae to write the poem (whilst leaning on the back of a fellow officer he penned this on a scrap piece of paper) that was to be immortalised when published in Punch. *McCrae would serve with great distinction until his death from pneumonia in January, 1918.*

> In Flanders fields, the poppies blow
> Between the crosses, row on row,
> That mark our place; and in the sky
> The larks, still bravely singing, fly
> Scarce heard amid the guns below.
> We are the Dead. Short days ago
> We lived, felt dawn, saw sunset glow,
> Loved, and were loved, and now we lie
> In Flanders fields.
> Take up our quarrel with the foe:
> To you from failing hands we throw
> The torch, be yours to hold it high.

If ye break faith with us who die
We shall not sleep, though poppies grow
In Flanders fields.

The poppy-wearing habit began in America, inspired by the poetry that emerged after the First World War. By the mid-1920s, poppies were being produced by disabled ex-servicemen on behalf of the Royal British Legion, formed in 1921 to ease the plight of veterans. Today each year in the run-up to 11 November, we see them being worn by people from all walks of life – each acting out there own tribute to the fallen of the Great War, and the conflicts that followed in the twentieth century.

THE GIRLS
Henry's daughters – Betty on the left, and Jean on the right – enjoying a day in the countryside c.1929.

DOWN ON THE FARM
Henry's family spent many happy times visiting friends and relatives in the Norfolk countryside – both his daughters loved horses.

DOWN ON THE FARM
Henry, with Betty and Jean on another visit to the countryside. Note the car, Henry was earning a relatively good living as a car mechanic to have his own vehicle, still a luxury in those days.

THE FAMILY

Henry's wife, Dorothy, with the girls – the family were close and Henry tried to spend as much time with them as possible, despite needing to earn money during the Depression of the 1930s.

ALL ABOARD

Henry's main relaxation was the sea. Here he is as skipper of his boat – *The Teale* – which he took out on daily trips with his family.

DAUGHTERS AT SEA

Henry encouraged both his children to love sailing as much as he did. Sadly he would later give up his boat when both daughters married and moved away after the war.

THE DAY JOB
Henry worked for many years at the Ford Motor Company in Dagenham – in an environment such as this one taken just before the war in 1939. (© Getty Images)

WORLD WAR TWO
With Hitler's Germany invading Poland in 1939, Britain was once again plunged into a European war. Henry would this time play a different – though just as vital – role. (© Getty Images)

A GERMAN MAGNETIC MIN
Henry would be part of the team
that worked round the clock on
finding a solution to combating
the problem of German magnetic
mines being dropped on our por
and shipping lanes in 1940. They
cracked the problem by investiga
a captured mine that was droppe
on an Essex sandbank near to wh
Henry actually lived and worked.
(© Getty Images)

JEAN ALLINGHAM
During the war both Jean and
Betty would brave the German
bombers to work in the capital.
Both worked in the civil service
and would be part of the support
teams that took part in historic
political meetings with the Allies
in 1943. (© David Gray)

GI BRIDE

LEFT: Jean's marriage to Lonny Gray – a tail-gunner in the USAAF – led to her relocating to America and to Henry's extended family setting up roots in a new country, as will be seen in later pictures.

BELOW: The family picture of Jean's wedding – Henry is fourth from the right hand side of the picture. (Both images © David Gray)

RETURNING HOME

Jean would return to visit her parents when she could – as seen here in the 1960s.

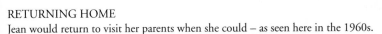

ALLINGHAMS GO WEST
Henry and Dorothy also took the chance to visit Jean in the USA and spent two happy visits in Michigan, where she lived, in the 1950s, and again in 1969. (© David Gray)

ON THE SEA AGAIN
Henry visiting his US-based family again in the 1990s – sailing with his grandson David Gray, and his great-grandson Christopher. (© David Gray)

FISHING IN THE USA
Henry enjoyed anything to do with water and took up many opportunities to take a boat out fishing – and here he's been lucky to get one! (© David Gray)

THE LOVING COUPLE
Henry and Dorothy enjoyed a long and loving marriage, and travelled everywhere together – such as on this cruise in 1968.

A RECIPE FOR GOOD HEALTH
Henry has maintained a healthy physical regime all of his life, playing golf until
he was 90 years old, and cycling on his 100th birthday.

HAPPY CENTURIAN
The loving relationship Henry enjoyed with Jean was seen in her joining him for his 100th birthday
party in 1996, sadly she died within a few years of this picture being taken aged 72 years old.

eight

CIVVY STREET

ON 19 MARCH 1919 I was discharged from the Royal Air Force at No. 1 Dispersal Unit in Purfleet and issued with a protection certificate and a certificate of identity. I gave my address as 5 Willow Road, Chadwell Heath, where Dorothy was staying with Uncle Charlie and Auntie Rosie. I also got a ration book. My demobilisation account shows I was earning three shillings a day. Of that I'd allocated two shillings and tuppence to Dorothy, leaving me with tenpence to live on.

After a total service amounting to 42 months and 26 days, my war gratuity worked out at £20 and 10s. With additional furlough pay and a rations and clothing allowance, I left the dispersal unit with the sum of £30, 7s and 8d. In addition I was awarded two medals, each one bearing my number, rank and name inscribed on the rim of the medal. These were the British War Medal 1914–20 and the Victory Medal.

Not every serviceman or woman who served in the armed services received a medal. Those who only saw service in the British Isles or other non-combative theatres of war were not issued with any. I did meet one such veteran who served in the Duke of Cornwall Light Infantry, whose military service was confined to Ireland. He would never join his fellow veterans at any events because he did not have a medal to prove he served in the First World War.

Henry was awarded two medals, each one bearing his number, rank and name inscribed on the rim of the medal. These were the British War Medal 1914–20 and the Victory Medal. The maximum number of medals issued to any one man or woman returning from the war was three, and only seven different medals were issued; these were:

- The 1914 Star – for those men who came under fire during the period 5 August to 22 November 1914

- The 1914–15 Star – for services in Flanders 23 November 1914 to 31 December 1915, to include East and West Africa, Gallipoli and Egypt

- British War Medals 1914–20

- Victory Medal

- The Mons Star – those men who fought at Mons were issued with a Star to pin on their 1914 medal ribbon

- Territorial Force Medal – for members of the Territorial Army prior to 30 September 1914

- Mercantile Marine War Medal – for the Merchant Navy 1914–18

Servicemen who were discharged as a result of sickness or wounds contracted or received during the war received, in addition to these medals, a circular silver war badge with the words: 'For King and Empire, services rendered.'

At the end of the war, the next of kin of those men and women who lost their lives during the conflict, or whose death was attributable to war service up to seven years after the war ended, were given a memorial plaque and a scroll bearing the name of the deceased. The plaques, made of bronze gun metal, were often referred to as 'dead men's pennies'. The words 'He died for freedom and honour' were inscribed around the edge and Britannia, with her trident, a wreath and lion, were depicted in the middle. Inscribed on the penny was the name of the dead man or woman. Deliberately, there was no insignia of rank. About 1,150,000 plaques were made and dispatched before the scheme came to an end.

Accompanying the penny was a scroll of darkened parchment, featuring the Royal Coat of Arms and the full name of the deceased, with a passage written in Old English script:

> He whom this scroll commemorates was numbered among those who, at the call of King and Country, left all that was dear to them, endured hardness, faced danger, and finally passed out of sight of men by the path of duty and self-sacrifice, giving up their own lives that others may live in freedom. Let those who come after see to it that his name be not forgotten.

There was also a letter signed by King George V that read:

> I join with my grateful people in sending you this memorial of a brave life given for others in the Great War.

Six and a half million silver war medals were minted. During the Great Depression many men were forced to sell the medals they were awarded after the First World War for scrap. The early post-war motto 'a land fit for heroes' was not a rallying cry that would help those men now on the economic scrapheap.

Almost immediately I got a job with a small aircraft company earning £4 a week. Dorothy and I were anxious to get a place of our own and, in April, we took a room with Mr and Mrs Ralph Goodmay in Romford. They had no children of their own and I think they became quite fond of us.

We spent most of that summer walking and talking. The work on aircraft assembly didn't challenge me so I handed in my notice. I was confident I would find another job but I wanted it to be the right job. Every morning I got on my bike and cycled off, looking for work.

One day I was crossing London using Rotten Row in Hyde Park when I saw a group of horsemen heading my way. I dismounted and waited for the group to pass. Then I realised King George V was leading the party. Instantly I doffed my cap and the King acknowledged the gesture by raising his whip. In an instant I shouted: 'Have you got a job for me, Sir? I wouldn't let you down.' But my words were drowned out by the clatter of hooves.

When Henry got a job, he considered himself one of the lucky ones. Soon a song, sung to the tune of 'It's a Long Way to Tipperary' was circulating among old soldiers who, having survived the war, found themselves down on their luck in civvy street.

> We won the war, what was it for?
> You can ask Lloyd George or Bonar Law
> We beat the Germans, the Austrians and the Turk,
> That's why we are all walking around, out of work.
> We won the war, what was it for?
> But next time the enemy's at your door,
> Take him in and shake his hand,
> Give him his dinner and treat him grand,
> What's the use of fighting any more?

In the end I joined Thorns Car Body Makers on piecework, paid for the amount of work costed and completed. When I earned £16 in a week I proudly gave it to Dorothy, warning her it was a one-off. She put £12 in the post office savings account.

In October 1921 we finally found a house of our own, a terraced property in Forest Gate, east London, at a controlled rent of five shillings per week. It was lit by gas lamps, had two bedrooms, a kitchen and a front room as well. The Goodmays were sad to see us go but Dorothy was already pregnant with our first child, Betty, and we needed a place of our own. Although the house had only one tap in the scullery with cold water, we thoroughly enjoyed it there. Dorothy – and later our two daughters, Betty and Jean – used a tin bath for bathing while I went to the municipal baths.

When I arrived home just before Christmas of 1926, I found the kitchen table covered with food. Dorothy quickly explained that Mrs Bell, the woman who helped her around the house sometimes, had not been able to afford Christmas food for herself and her family. I guessed the Bells were suffering in the Great Depression, like many other families. I helped Dorothy carry the food around to the Bells and they were very pleased to see us. I was proud of Dorothy and her kindness to others.

While we were there an Alsatian bitch, heavy with pup, ambled into the room.

'Come back and have the choice of the litter,' Mr Bell said, as he was anxious to give us something in return.

'The children have been asking for a puppy for months,' I said to Dorothy. 'Why don't we do that?'

After the pups were born I was too busy to visit the Bells and told her she must make the choice.

'But I don't know anything about dogs. How will I know which to pick?'

I told her to stand some distance from the mother and choose the first puppy that made its way over to her. That's how we got Pamela. We all loved Pamela but soon she became my dog. I cannot tell you how much pleasure that dog gave me over the years. I took control of her training and her obedience and once I even took her to a dog show where she was 'highly commended'. The day Pamela died I hid myself away from everyone and sobbed.

In 1927 I got friendly with a tenant farmer in Leytonstone called Rob. We used to go rabbit shooting together on his land and I helped out when I could. Rob rewarded me with plenty of vegetables. He was also friendly with a neighbouring dairy farmer's daughter called Romma.

One day there was a knock on the door and Romma and Rob stood before me, she looking dishevelled. They told me Romma's mother had decided she was neglecting her chores because of her association with Rob so she had hidden all her daughter's clothes and ended her allowance. Rob had little money as every penny he earned went back into the farm. They stood before me and asked for my help.

'Are you serious about Romma?' I asked Rob, and he nodded.

'And you, Romma,' I said. 'Do you want to leave your family?' In a quiet voice she said, 'Yes.'

The next day Romma went shopping with Dorothy to replace her missing clothes. And soon the pair were married at the register office with myself and Dorothy as witnesses.

I went through a few jobs in the motor industry. It was a boom industry although cars were still primitive. A car owner could get straight into his newly purchased car with no tuition and drive it away. But cars were notoriously unreliable. Nobody would venture on a long journey without a toolbox, valves, springs, spark plugs and other spare parts. There were many more hazards on the road than today, including the inexperience of first-time drivers and horse-drawn vehicles. It was difficult to judge speed and dogs were forever pursuing vehicles. You had to double declutch to get going. It was worse in winter when you really had to wrap up warmly. Some motorists I saw had more layers on than when I first went flying in 1915.

But, as the production of war materials ended, so factories were looking for new goods to manufacture and cars were it. Typically, cars were open tourers with four seats, running boards and a fixed starting handle. They had wheels with wooden spokes and three-inch pressure tyres. At first there were no windscreen wipers and the lamps were fuelled by oil. Initially, brakes were put only on the rear wheels, although front-wheel brakes became standard in 1923. The roads, stones and potholes made for bumpy rides.

Every time I changed jobs I got more money, but I was always concerned that my lack of qualifications was holding me back. I joined Barkers in Latimer Road, Newham, which made Royal coaches. Then I went to another firm of coach-builders in Cambridge Heath, Hackney. This firm was run by two brothers, Willie and Bronco Wells. Bronco won his nickname because he always wore a Stetson hat. Work included making vehicle bodies for the bullion vans run by the Bank of England. When I left them, the brothers wrote to me to say there would always be a job there for me.

After that I worked for Vickers General Motors on piecework. I barely saw the girls during that period. But when Vickers moved to Weybridge in Surrey, Dorothy and I decided to stay put as the girls were happy at school. I knew I'd soon find more work. After all, by now I had to feed the cat, the dog, nine hens, two girls and my Dorothy.

This time I joined H.J.M. Car Body Builders and got a salary for the first time. The company was linked to the building of vehicles for Bentleys, Mercedes, Rolls Royce and other manufacturers. Often the cars were tested at Brooklands racetrack in Weybridge and I thoroughly enjoyed my visits there.

The working day started at 8 a.m. and finished at 5.30 p.m. There was no overtime. Some of our best customers were the Maharajas of India who demanded personal specifications. I can remember the Maharaja of Alwa coming to buy a Rolls Royce at a price of £40,000. Although he admired the car, the Maharaja wanted a vehicle from which he could shoot game. I suggested a sliding roof would fill the bill. I think this was one of the earliest examples of a sun roof.

While I was at H.J.M. I visited the Rolls Royce plant with my managing director. We were being shown around an assembly line when one of a group of engineers limped up to me.

'It's Henry Allingham, is it not?' he asked, pumping my outstretched hand vigorously. 'You won't remember me. We were at St Pol together in 12 Squadron. You looked after my Sopwith.'

I was searching my memory when he added, 'I'm sure we flew together.'

Still examining my mind for his name, I asked him about his limp.

'Yes, it happened soon after you left. I crash landed just inside our lines. I escaped with my life but lost a leg.' Now he was in charge of the production line at Rolls Royce – but I still couldn't recall his name.

A few years before this I had bumped into the pilot who was with me on HMT *Kingfisher* during the Battle of Jutland. He, too, had lost a limb, his arm. Again, the meeting was brief. It was at Turnham Green tube station and the crowds soon parted us, so I never found out what had happened to his arm.

But at the time, people hardly ever talked about the war. If someone was about the same age as you, well, you assumed they had seen action but it was never a topic for conversation. People just didn't want to talk about such painful subjects, better to forget and move forward.

Determined to keep up with the rapid technological advances of the time, I joined Ford Motor Company at Dagenham in 1934, designing new car bodies. Ford's opened in Dagenham in 1931 after re-locating from Trafford, Manchester. It was the era when metal was replacing wood for car bodies and it was part of my job to oversee this work. For the first time I realised that my qualifications were fine as I had chartered engineers reporting directly to me.

I made sure the girls had a great childhood. They were both 'outdoors' types, and rode bicycles and horses. Both of them played tennis very well to a standard that they knocked up with all the players who went to the Wimbledon Championships. They got equipment from Slazenger – three of everything for the price of one. But sadly, I never saw them play. I was always too busy. I sometimes worked long hours. When the work was there I made the most of it as you never knew what could be around the corner after the Depression of the 1920s.

Dorothy had one brother, Bernard, who was four years younger than me, and two sisters, Ivy and Lilly. Her father was called Noah. In 1928 I bought a cottage for Noah in Norfolk and helped him to renovate it. The garden was some two acres, which allowed Noah to be self-sufficient. I also paid the tithe fees, even though I felt the Church had enough money of its own. But Noah was a deeply religious man who was generous with his contributions to the Church. Dorothy and the children spent many summer holidays in the cottage. I would drive them to the cottage in our Austin Seven. Whenever we visited Noah, we always returned in a car loaded with fresh vegetables and fruit.

In about 1933 I came home with the news that I had a week's leave and discussed with Dorothy the prospect of going somewhere. Dorothy quickly pointed out that both Betty and Jean were approaching their end-of-term examinations and had to stay at school.

Dorothy suggested I should go and stay with Noah and do some fishing. It was a marvellous week. We lived off the land, netted many eels and ate them. The early crop of peas was always high on the menu. Every evening ended in a singsong. I always had a soft spot for Norfolk and thought that one day I would retire there. It was in Norfolk that I had met and married Dorothy and had spent many happy holidays with the Cater family. Dorothy, however, had set her mind on Eastbourne, and when Noah died, she sold the cottage.

In 1938 I was elected a member of the Narrow Seas Club, which had been founded in 1932. I remained a member until 1953, sailing my four-ton sloop, the *Teal*. The object of the club, as stated in its rules, was 'to provide facilities for social intercourse among men interested in the handling of small craft'. The membership was restricted to 250 with an annual subscription of five shillings (25 pence). [The Narrow Seas of the club's title is a term that has fallen out of use but refers to the waters separating England from France and Ireland. The club room, at that time, was The Old Ship, Ivy Lane, in the City of London.] I'd been lucky. Boats had always been a part of my life as my grandfather and Uncle Charlie both rowed before the war, and I loved being on the water. Dorothy was not too keen on sailing but Jean took to it with the same enthusiasm as me. The *Teal* was moored at Burnham-on-Crouch in Essex and it was in this area that I did most of my sailing.

nine

THE SECOND WORLD WAR

EVERYONE COULD SEE THE Second World War was coming from the late 1930s – Hitler couldn't be trusted and we shouldn't have allowed him to get away with what he did. When war broke out in September 1939, I was 43 years old and I felt acclimatised to it already. I thought about enlisting but it wasn't going to happen. I had never considered myself a soldier fighter and I thought my contribution would be in the same vein as before. In fact, I was served with a 'works essential' order, which meant I had to stay in my job due to its importance. I couldn't change employer and I couldn't join the services. The decision was made for me and Dorothy said, 'At least they can't send you into this war.' It spared her the pain of me being away again.

On Christmas Day 1939 I was halfway through my Christmas dinner with my family when someone from Ford's knocked on the door and told me to report back to the factory immediately. I just about had time to finish my dinner and say goodbye to Dorothy, Betty and Jean. I had no idea what was happening.

When I arrived at the factory I discovered that the German

Luftwaffe had dropped a new type of magnetic mine in Harwich harbour, preventing ships from moving in or out. The British had no minesweeping countermeasures at the time. Mines laid by Germany could paralyse the nation and so damage our ability to keep the country going with foodstuffs as well as raw materials for armaments. With U-boats lurking in the open seas and harbours littered with mines, Britain would soon have been isolated and strangled of supplies.

Fortunately, one of the mines had been dropped in the mud flats at Shoeburyness, in Southend-on-Sea, Essex. My team had to develop a magnetic sweep that would trigger the mine so it could explode harmlessly. We also designed a mantle that allowed ships to pass safely over a bed of mines without activating the firing mechanism.

It was the longest week of my life. I had very little sleep and felt under immense pressure. By the beginning of the New Year, the harbour was cleared of all mines and open for shipping – and myself and the rest of the team were finally allowed to go home. Although I think about 50 ships, including a destroyer, were sunk by magnetic mines during the war, we made them largely ineffective. Once the war had ended, again I could look back on the period and what I had achieved with some satisfaction. What we had worked on was vital to allow our country to fight and win the war against the Nazis.

The U-boat fleet, which dominated much of the battle of the Atlantic, was small at the beginning of the war and much of the early action by German forces involved mining convoy routes and ports around Britain. The German submarines also operated in the Mediterranean Sea, in the Caribbean Sea, and along the North American coast.

Initially contact mines were employed – meaning that a ship had to physically strike a mine to detonate it – usually tethered at the end of a cable just below the surface of the water. By the beginning of the Second World War most nations had developed mines that could be dropped from aircraft and floated on the surface, making it possible to lay them in enemy harbours. The use of dredging and nets was effective against this type of mine, but this consumed time and resources, and required harbours to be closed. Contact mines usually hole a ship's hull. Later some ships survived mine blasts, limping into port with buckled plates and broken backs. This appeared to be due to a new type of mine, detecting ships magnetically and detonating at a distance, causing damage with the shock wave of the explosion. Ships that had successfully run the gauntlet of the Atlantic crossing were sometimes destroyed entering freshly cleared British harbours. More shipping was being lost than could be replaced, and Churchill ordered that the intact recovery of one of these new mines was of the highest priority.

As Henry recalls, the British experienced a stroke of luck in November 1939 when a German mine was dropped from an aircraft onto the mud flats of the Thames estuary during low tide. As if this were not sufficiently good fortune, the land belonged to the Army, and a base with men and workshops was at hand. Experts were dispatched from London to investigate the mine. They had some idea that the mines used magnetic sensors, so everyone removed all metal, including their buttons, and made tools of non-magnetic brass. They disarmed the mine and rushed it to labs at Portsmouth, where scientists discovered a new type of arming mechanism. A large ferrous object passing through the Earth's magnetic field will concentrate the field through it; the mine's detector was designed to trigger at the mid-point of a steel-hulled ship passing overhead. The mechanism had an adjustable sensitivity, calibrated in milligauss.

From these data, methods were developed to clear the mines. Early methods included the use of large electromagnets dragged behind ships or below low-flying aircraft (a number of older bombers like the

Vickers Wellington were used for this). Both these methods had the disadvantage of 'sweeping' only a small strip. A better solution was found in the 'Double-L Sweep' using electrical cables dragged behind ships that passed large pulses of current through the seawater. This induced a large magnetic field and swept the entire area between the two ships. The older methods continued to be used in smaller areas. The Suez Canal continued to be swept by aircraft, for instance. The work Henry and the team he was with undertook proved invaluable in the fight to win control of the sea, as well as keep British harbours open for shipping throughout the war.

At the time we lived in Boundary Road, Plaistow, in east London. As soon as the war started, I bought 32 pieces of 1/16 ply. This was to cover the windows for the blackout, so that houses couldn't be seen by German planes allowing them to either bomb you, or use your location as a guide to their intended targets. It also stopped the cold getting in!

I also put up an Anderson shelter, which was made of corrugated steel and took up most of the garden. There were no direct hits in our neighbourhood but the shelter protected us from shrapnel and other bomb fragments that were scattered across the area.

At the beginning of the war I worked with Malcolm Campbell and his son Donald at Ford's in Dagenham. I think Malcolm Campbell (1885–1948) was a director. He won nine land speed records between 1924 and 1935 as well as four water speed records. But it was his son Donald (1921–1967) whom I got to know well. He had volunteered for the Royal Air Force when war broke out, but was rejected when the medics found he had suffered rheumatic fever as a child. He worked for Briggs Motor Bodies, which liaised with Ford's and Rolls Royce. He was assigned to my section and I often spent time with him during lunch breaks where we'd chat about various subjects – he was great company. Unfortunately, he died in 1967 following a 320-mph crash, trying to break another speed record in his boat *Bluebird* on Coniston Water in the Lake District. He was a brave and driven man, and it has been fascinating seeing his boat being reclaimed from Coniston after all these years.

Employment at Ford's went from 12,000 to 35,000 during the Second World War. I've discovered since that the plant turned out 360,000 military vehicles, light vans, army trucks, mobile canteens and Bren gun carriers, as well as 95 per cent of wartime tractors. More important still were the 250,000 V8 engines.

Both my girls were coming out of their teens at this time and so wanted to build careers for themselves. With manpower in short supply there was a variety of occupations opening to them. Betty got a good job in the Foreign Office while Jean was in the Colonial Office – both situated in the centre of London. They used to take the train into east London as the Underground ran from East Ham, then they walked to work from there. It was worrying when the Germans were bombing the capital, but everyone just got on with life as best they could. Betty had the distinction of accompanying the Prime Minister – Winston Churchill – during the key summit meetings that were held in Casablanca in 1943 where the invasion of Sicily was planned, and then Tehran in the same year where the Big Three all met for the first time – Churchill, Roosevelt and 'Uncle Joe' Stalin.

The summit held in Casablanca, Morocco, in January 1943 was attended by Churchill and American President Franklin D. Roosevelt. They were joined by leading Free French Generals Charles de Gaulle and Henri Giraud. The Russian leader Stalin was invited but declined to go.

When the summit finished, Roosevelt announced the war would only end with the 'unconditional surrender' of Germany and Japan.

Almost simultaneously, British General Bernard Montgomery took Tripoli in northern Africa from the Germans, and within a week the German Army in Stalingrad surrendered, its first major defeat.

At the end of the year, a major conference in Tehran, Iran, attracted Stalin as well as Churchill and Roosevelt. It was here that Stalin found out about Operation Overlord, the plan to open a second front in Europe by an Allied invasion of France – news he greeted gladly, knowing this would alleviate pressure on his troops fighting on the Eastern Front.

I had a car, as I received a special allowance. I paid £20 for it when it was five weeks old, a General Motors job. I sold it for £200 after the war. It was an old banger by then. I could have got £400 for it if I'd wanted to, but I was never greedy. You couldn't buy anything after the war, for love nor money.

Food was rationed so I decided to buy a Remington Repeater rifle with telescopic sights and go rabbiting. First I had to convince the police that I was a fit and proper person to own a rifle, then I got the necessary gun licence. I hunted for rabbits in nearby Epping Forest and provided meat for our own table and for friends and neighbours. I never let Dorothy skin the rabbits. It was no job for a lady.

Once I was invited by a local farmer to take part in a deer shoot in the uplands of Epping. Three deer were culled and I was taught how to skin and bone the carcasses. I was rewarded with quite a bit of venison, which provided for many meals.

People like me served as home guards, air-raid wardens, auxiliary firemen or helped in hospitals. I chose to work in King George Hospital in Romford, Essex, where I was responsible for a team of stretcher-bearers as well as directing incoming casualties to different locations for treatment. I used to work there from 5 p.m. on Saturdays to 7 a.m. on Sundays. One of the worst jobs I had to do was help in the identification of 400 men, women and children whose bodies were temporarily stored in West Ham Municipal Baths during the Blitz.

One problem for Londoners was the threat of unexploded bombs, which littered the streets after a raid. One morning a street was closed off because of an unexploded bomb. I couldn't be bothered to walk all the way around the block so I cut across the tape. A policeman at the other end of the street saw me and was just starting to tell me off when the bomb exploded – luckily no one was injured. Another bomb that was detonated in our neighbourhood blew out the windows and dislodged tiles at our family home.

In 1944 Betty met and married a naval officer – Roland. The wedding reception was held in the Roebuck Hotel in Woodford. Although food was rationed, I called in a lot of favours to cater for 150 guests. There was a toastmaster and a professional dance band. That evening I turned to Dorothy and said, 'Well, we have kept the promise we made when we got married. Betty and Roland wanted for nothing on their wedding day.'

When Henry awoke on his 48th birthday, on 6 June 1944, it was to news that the invasion of France had begun. His birthday became better known as D-Day and the country, and indeed much of the world, celebrated this auspicious occasion with him.

The campaign to free Europe from the grip of the Nazis was perhaps the worst-kept secret in Britain. Military bases, especially those by the coast, had been thronging with servicemen from Britain, the Commonwealth and America. New airfields had been built, extra railway tracks laid down and the nation's harbours re-organised for the scores of necessary ships. Everyone knew something was brewing. They even knew relevant code words that were bandied about by troops and some officers. But no one bar a select few knew precisely where or when the action would happen. Indeed, the Germans – aware that an invasion was in the offing – were convinced the onslaught would come on the coast near Calais, not least because of a sprawling fake army camp established on the Kent shoreline. But suddenly troops, ships and aircraft were gone, and were fighting on the beaches of Normandy rather than the Pas-de-Calais, in some of the bloodiest confrontations of the conflict.

The momentous event had been planned for 5 June, the day before Henry's birthday. The date had been selected by the military's top brass for its happy combination of low dawn tides and late rising moon. However, the weather was so treacherously poor that it would have jeopardised the entire operation. A 24-hour delay was agreed, although the weather the following day remained far from fair. Commanders felt that another delay would effectively shelve for several weeks invasion plans that had taken years to perfect.

Thus, on 6 June 1944, 1,200 fighting ships, 4,126 landing craft and 804 transport ships, plus assorted other vessels, blackened the sea off Normandy. Some 10,000 military aircraft were in the sky or preparing for take-off. Aboard the Allied ships were 132,000 young men whose task it was to begin the liberation of Europe by gaining a foothold on the beaches. Most were queasy with seasickness, having been penned aboard for some time as their commanders waited for the gales to abate.

Some 23,500 American and British troops had already been parachuted beyond the coastline before dawn broke. A belief among German defenders that this was a diversion, with the real invasion destined to occur on the coast at Calais, was soon shattered.

American soldiers headed for beaches code-named 'Utah' and 'Omaha' while the British and Commonwealth troops were targeting beaches code-named 'Sword', 'Juno' and 'Gold'. The most deadly resistance came on 'Omaha' beach, where battle-hardened Germans fresh from the brutalities of the Eastern Front had taken up positions just weeks before. Although the final death toll is unclear, it is thought that 2,500 American soldiers died before D-Day came to an end.

The success of D-Day was far from certain. The campaign could have stalled at any time or even ended in disaster. But at the close of what has since been dubbed 'the longest day', there were about 155,000 Allied troops ashore. Although many of the military objectives were unfulfilled, progress was being made. On the evening of Henry's birthday, Winston Churchill made a speech in the House of Commons.

> This vast operation is undoubtedly the most complicated and difficult that has ever taken place . . . There are already hopes that actual tactical surprise has been attained and we hope to furnish the enemy with a succession of surprises during the course of the fighting. The battle that has now begun will grow constantly in scale and in intensity for many weeks to come and I shall not attempt to speculate upon its course.

My daughter Jean, meanwhile, had met a gunner with the 8th US Army Air Force, named Lonny Gray, while she was on holiday in Scotland. They were married on 2 April 1945 in Woodford Wells, Essex.

At the end of the war, Lonny returned to a job in the City Engineering Department in Grand Rapids, Michigan, where his father was assistant engineer. Jean subsequently followed her husband to America once all her paperwork was in order, in 1946 – a 'GI Bride' as they say, and I lost not only a daughter and companion but also a valuable crew member. With both daughters having married, I decided to sell the *Teal* and spend more of my leisure time with Dorothy. Subsequent visits to America invariably involved sailing with my grandchildren, though, who named one of their boats after me. Five years later, Dorothy and I went to

America for a visit, to be reunited with Jean and Lonny and to meet our three-year-old grandson, David Lee Gray, for the first time. More of him later.

During the Suez Crisis, Ford shares fell in price to about ten shillings from a high of £3. I bought as many as I could lay my hands on.

Henry's service medals were lost during the Second World War. It never seemed to bother him that when he attended ceremonial events, he was not able to display any medals. He refused to replace them with miniature medals, which had been produced for sale later in the twentieth century. There were occasions when Henry was loaned the relevant medals, but often they had to be secured to his jacket by the use of safety pins and swiftly skewed. Subsequently, when he appeared in newspapers and on television in recent years, Henry looked scruffy. The Royal Navy became aware of Henry's plight and arranged for the medals in question to be replaced. The two medals he wears now are unique and special. No other First World War veteran has had his medals replaced by the Government. To distinguish them from other medals, the word 'replacement' appears on the rim of the medals, alongside his name and rank.

ten

POST-WAR LIFE

WORKING LIFE CONTINUED MUCH as it always had after the end of the Second World War – I am the same as every other working man and woman in that I led an ordinary life after the war – you just got on with it. I used to entertain foreign buyers and I had to persuade Dorothy that she could be a great hostess. Life at home settled into an enjoyable routine. I would never let Dorothy cook Sunday lunch, just as I wouldn't dream of asking her to skin any of the rabbits I shot. It was no job for a woman.

But it wasn't all work, work, work. I learned to dance and bought myself a piano. Remembering the promise I had made to myself during the First World War, I started working towards music exams. Unfortunately, the teacher who was giving me lessons got an offer to work in America and disappeared. I didn't take any more tuition after that.

I still never spoke to anyone about the Great War. Dorothy and I became very friendly with another couple and we met at each other's houses once or twice a week to play whist. This happened for at least five years. The wives found out from each other that their husbands had both served in the war. But Dorothy didn't mention it to me until years later, after they had moved away. If you'd served in the Great War, you just never spoke about it.

When I came up to retirement in 1961 – just as they were gearing up for production of the Cortina at Dagenham – we put a deposit on a new flat in Eastbourne. It took two years for it to be completed. We moved in during 1964 and we loved it there. My pension on retirement was £2, 17s and 6d.

I used to do a lot of fishing with a mate called Sid Grey. One day, when we were fishing off the pier, Sid didn't react quickly enough when there was a sudden jerk from beneath the waves and his best rod disappeared under the water. But two hours later, Sid got another bite. He landed his catch and found it was his best rod with a whopper on the end of it. I didn't win any prize fish – but I did provide something for our tea.

We went to America twice, once in the 1950s and again in 1969, to see Jean and her family. I liked America and they would have liked us to stay. But there is no place like England. This is my country and this is where I want to be.

Dorothy died of leukaemia in 1970 when I was 74 years old. I scattered her ashes on the South Downs and in the promenade gardens at Eastbourne – she had been my lifelong companion. After Dorothy's death, I often went to Norfolk, as it was there I had met and married Dorothy and enjoyed many happy holidays with the Cater family, especially with Noah, my father-in-law, and Bernard, my brother-in-law, who was only four years younger than me.

I suffered from a hernia during the 1970s. At that time I had an up-and-over garage door. I was stretching to reach the door when I felt it go. The hernia was repaired in hospital, which proved to be a surprisingly sociable place. Just before I left, I got a message that the ward sister wanted to see me. I thought she had a rocket for me because I had been exercising soon after the operation.

'On the contrary,' she said. 'I want to thank you for what you did, not only for the patients on the ward but also the doctors and nurses.' I suppose she meant that I had kept everybody's spirits up. She offered me a sherry and we arranged to have a game of golf.

Golf was a big feature of my later life. I played golf for 35 years, ultimately with a handicap of eight. On holidays I toured the country and played golf at some of the best courses in the country, including Gleneagles. Of course, I did this alone, driving myself. I was happy being on my own as I was always a bit of a loner. I stopped playing golf when I was 93. Until then I had got around without a stick, no trouble. I didn't let anyone know how old I was and nobody guessed. But I could keep up with everybody else there. Then my sight left me and I couldn't hit a ball properly. When I left my golf club for the last time, I didn't say goodbye to anyone, I just went.

Dorothy and I used to play cards together a lot. Never on a Sunday, though, or for money. Later I took up bridge, which I loved when I could see and hear properly. Then I became a pain in the neck to other people when my sight and hearing went. I didn't want to spoil their pleasure.

When I couldn't read number plates any more, I had to give up driving. I gave my two-litre Ford Cortina to the local hospice and I bought myself a mountain bike. I used to get up at 5 a.m. and cycle over the South Downs before the traffic got busy. There is a picture of me still cycling at the age of 100. I never wore a cycle helmet, just a baseball cap sent to me from my family in America.

Although the prospect of a new century excited most people, it had little effect on my life. I was still living alone in my flat in Eastbourne and I managed pretty well. In the morning I made my own breakfast, usually a Weetabix with raisins, and bread or toast with marmalade. My midday meal was delivered from a local residential home. In the evening I got myself what I fancied. Steak remained a favourite, which I cooked after knocking it about with a kitchen hammer. Usually I followed my tea with a banana. Once a week I caught the Age Concern bus to a local supermarket to do my shopping. Otherwise, I kept myself to myself. I was still trying to forget everything that had gone on during the war.

I divided my day roughly into two twelve-hour periods, getting up at about 6.30 a.m. and going to bed at about 6.30 p.m. Perhaps I didn't need that much sleep but I felt the bed rest was just as important as getting about during the daytime.

Often, during the night, I would get up to raid the fridge for a drink, a chocolate, a biscuit or a banana. I used to call this 'sips'. I still look forward to sips today and, even better, if I stay at a hotel or with the Goodwins, it is usually provided on my bedside table.

For 20 years I had a companion for friendship and we had lunch together every Sunday. I used to call her 'Hockey Sticks'. Obviously, when you are more than 100 years old, the number of people you have known for years and can count as friends diminishes. And I was a loner – I didn't make many friends in the first place.

eleven

RESURRECTION

IN 1987 DENNIS GOODWIN and his son Stephen founded the World War One Veterans' Association after observing care available to this generation of men. In his professional life, Stephen Goodwin was responsible for the registration of residential care homes in the north-west of England. Meanwhile, Dennis was a lay inspector of residential homes in West Sussex. Both men saw the problems of loneliness and isolation among the elderly, especially the men, who were substantially outnumbered by women. However, these men had one thing in common, as all had experienced the trauma of the First World War while the women and staff had little perception of what life had really been like at the Somme, Passchendaele, Gallipoli and Verdun. Although the men received plenty of tender, loving care in their homes, this single linking factor was not being addressed.

'I was saddened at the way survivors of the 1914–18 war were being shunted into nursing and residential homes and while there seemed to be an abundance of TLC there was a scarcity of any awareness or recognition of the significance of the lives of these men both during

this horrendous war of attrition and the subsequent years as they battled to build a future for themselves and their families during the Depression of the 1920s. For those who fought at Mons, the Somme, Passchendaele, Gallipoli and Arras, how could their histories and the horrors they went through be ignored, or brushed under the carpet now they were old men. Men simply retreated into their own shell hole of memories as the effects of benign institutionalism eroded their willingness to fight the ravages of the ageing process.'

Few of the men involved had returned to the killing fields of Flanders since the conflict and wondered if it was possible. Dennis and Stephen decided to remedy that situation by organising a trip. Stephen brought seven old soldiers down from the north-west while Dennis enlisted a further seven from his home town of Rustington, West Sussex.

'I found that they were simple ordinary men who were placed in extraordinary circumstances,' explained Dennis. 'It is the camaraderie and sense of fun and adventure that depicts the best of them I think, and that they all believed that their "little bit" in the Great War was insignificant, when of course this wasn't true at all.'

Before they left for Europe, there was a reception for the men on the south coast, starting at 7 p.m. It was almost two hours later, to much relief from those already assembled, that the north-west contingent wheeled and shuffled in one by one, to be greeted by spontaneous applause. No one was more relieved than Dennis – who harboured grave misgivings on the outcome of the trip – as he viewed the veterans and their many physical disabilities. He thought to himself, 'Well Steve, you might have got them this far, but I doubt we can get them across the Channel, let alone survive a week in France.'

But soon he fell into conversation with Dick Trafford, who had joined up aged 15, was wounded on the Somme and survived the horrors of Passchendaele. Dick told how the soldiers had received a wonderful send-off from Lancashire, led by the Lord Mayor, a brass band and the cheers of local schoolchildren.

'Mind you,' Dick said, 'don't say anything to your Stephen but during the journey in the minibus, I haven't been so shaken up since the German bombardments of the trenches.'

Two of the 14 were terminally ill, one had grave communication problems and another was wheelchair-bound. However, the old soldiers closed ranks and supported one another.

'On this particular pilgrimage, as with others, these old soldiers found a new lease of life,' explained Dennis. 'They started to use limbs they had long given up. On the last evening in France, a veteran who was almost monosyllabic left everyone else speechless as he joined in the old songs of 1914 to 1918. That morning, the man in his wheelchair had been left on his own away from the group in the dining room of the hotel we were in, and he crawled over to the group accompanied by shouts of support.'

The pilgrimage was reported by the Sunday Telegraph, which printed Dennis' name and telephone number. He was overwhelmed by calls and the World War One Veterans'Association was born. Recently retired, Dennis readily accepted the challenge of running an organisation dedicated to the dwindling band of First World War veterans. He built up a network of helpers and wrote regular newsletters.

'That pilgrimage was a catalyst really. The effect on these veterans was both startling and remarkable. These quite frail men, handicapped and bearing the effects of the ageing process, some who had lost direction and purpose in life, shrugged off their disabilities and found an inner strength as they strove to compete with one another to walk tall in the face of the inordinate amount of interest shown to them by the public and media alike. Many, many soldiers had lost life and limbs in Flanders 70 years ago but on this occasion almost all found a new lease of life.

'It was this transformation of their physical and mental condition that put me on the spot, and when the phone kept ringing with messages *that 'my husband, father, grandfather, uncle, brother had never been back to Flanders,' and would I take them – that is when I realised we had opened up a Pandora's Box. The more times I took them, the more these men got under my skin and into my life on a daily basis. Indeed, it became a way of life for me as I formed more and more friendships and they became almost like surrogate fathers to me, and my own family slipped into this newly found extended family.*

'Although this is very much a family effort of not just the wider Goodwin clan but also the families of those veterans who belong to the association, we all feel the same responsibility of not only caring for these men, but also their legacy and the message they all want to convey. We hope we have demolished the barriers between age and youth, ability and disability and the past and the future. I hold a key role; if anything goes wrong I am the one responsible.'

With his contacts among veterans, Dennis heard about Henry in the new millennium and began visiting him at his flat in Eastbourne. Henry's daughter Jean had recently died and that had hit him hard. He had given away all his memorabilia to his family in America and was literally waiting to die. Despite Dennis' best efforts, Henry consistently made it plain he did not wish to be reminded of the war. However, Dennis maintained contact and, during a visit on a warm day in 2002, finally propelled him outside in his wheelchair for the first time.

'The sun was cracking the flagstones and the heat was making the flat uncomfortable,' Dennis recalled. 'But until now Henry had always refused to come outside the flat with me. I was acting on impulse when I said, "It's too warm in here, let's go down to the garden." I was out of the door and heading for the lift before Henry could muster opposition. We both blinked when we were outside, Henry because of the sun and me because I had been so audacious. It took me many visits and conversations with Henry over many weeks and months to win his confidence but

equally to get him into a positive frame of mind that there was a world out there that wanted to meet him and hear his stories.'

Dennis wheeled Henry along the promenade towards the pier, hearing about Henry's many memories of the resort. The next day the veteran rang Dennis to say he had enjoyed the best night's sleep he could remember. It was the start of a friendship that blossomed as Henry's sight, hearing and mobility diminished.

Dennis continued to visit my flat and together we went to visit fellow veterans, especially those close to our south-coast homes, in Sussex, Kent and Surrey. These meetings with other men who had witnessed similar events and horrors to me began to change my decision never to talk about what had gone on during the war. Those who had fought in the trenches had seen more than their fair share of the horrors of war. Gradually it seemed more disrespectful to ignore what had gone on than to talk about it.

I began welcoming students and researchers into my home to talk about what had gone on. Dennis acted as my eyes and ears as my sight and hearing were by now fading fast.

Suddenly my diary was full of events and I began meeting the forces' top brass and even royalty. I started talking to schoolchildren about my experiences in the war. It all gave me a reason to get up in the morning. I was the subject of films and photographs galore. All I heard was 'just one more, Henry.' If only I had a pound for every time that has been said to me, I'd be a rich man.

At Christmas 2002 Dennis decided a hamper of groceries would be a suitable gift for Henry, knowing that such gestures were popular with veterans. He wheeled Henry around a large supermarket, asking what his choice of foodstuffs would be. Henry said he could do with some marmalade.

'What brand do you usually have, Henry,' Dennis asked.

'Dulchie,' came the reply.

'I've never heard of it,' Dennis said, as he scoured the shelves. Almost every brand was passed to Henry for his inspection and each was rejected, some with more scorn than others.

'Marmalade is marmalade,' Dennis said, with increasing exasperation. Henry replied, 'I only have Dulchie and nothing else will do.'

Dennis spotted an assistant and sought her advice. The assistant moved further down the shelves and produced a jar of marmalade from the Duchy of Cornwall, quite a lot more expensive than other brands.

Then Dennis asked Henry about biscuits. Henry paddled his wheelchair nearer to the shelves, completely ignoring all the packet varieties. He chose a large tin of shortbread that exceeded every other biscuit on the shelves in terms of price, regardless of quality.

'What about a bottle of wine?' Dennis asked, picking up a £5 bottle of red wine and handing it to Henry.

'Plonk,' came Henry's disdainful comment. 'What I'd like is a good Burgundy.'

The price moved ever higher until he found what he termed a reasonable wine. A few more basic items of food were selected without comment but Dennis was growing anxious because the cost of the trolley full of food in front of him was getting way past his price limit of £20. His thoughts were interrupted by Henry saying, 'I hope they have strawberries here. Let's go and have a look.'

Strawberries they did have and at a price that reflected their rarity in the winter. Henry was in full flow about the wonderful advances being made in the food industry, observing, 'There is no such thing now as non-seasonal fruit or vegetables. Modern technology has provided produce making all markets accessible worldwide.'

Dennis moved very rapidly to the checkout before Henry could add any more to the luxury hamper.

At the beginning of 2003 there were 29 known veterans from the First World War. Although many members had died, there were still people coming forward to fill the depleting ranks. Two new recruits appeared. One was Nicholas Swarbrick, who was two years younger than me and had served as a radio operator in the Merchant Navy. A teetotaller, he had remained unmarried. He lived at Grimsargh, near Preston, and had managed to keep his personal history a secret for many years. I went on the long journey north with Dennis but it was well worth it. Nicholas and I had lots to talk about.

The other new recruit was Andrew Rigby, who lived in Lancing, West Sussex, close to my own home. He had joined the Lancashire Fusiliers aged 13 as a mule boy. We got on extremely well. His sheltered housing complex became a regular stopover for Dennis and me.

Merchant seaman Nicholas Swarbrick, who died on 2 February 2006 aged 107, served as a radio officer on Atlantic convoys. Aged six when his mother died from tuberculosis, he went to a Catholic school in Preston. As his home was next door to the local railway station, he would watch for the steam train to pull up at the platform before he left the house. He enjoyed school until, at the age of 14, he was severely beaten by one of the priests for a homework misdemeanour. After the shocking incident, he never returned to school again.

When the First World War broke out, he was working for his father. He seized the chance to take a course in Liverpool learning Morse Code and was subsequently commissioned as a radio officer on the SS Westfalia. His first sailing was to Halifax, Nova Scotia, to bring back horses for the cavalry on the Western Front. In December 1917, his ship left Halifax just before a munitions ship exploded, killing more than 2,000 people and destroying much of the port.

German U-boats were wreaking havoc with Allied shipping, sending thousands of service personnel, and civilians, to the seabed. Much later, Mr Swarbrick told how he learned first when ships had been hit:

> As radio officer I could hear the SOS messages from torpedoed ships, ships in distress and going down, and hearing their death throes. It was pretty horrifying to hear what was happening on the airwaves. And the instruction we had was not to go to their aid, because you yourself then became a target for the sub lurking close by. You had to get the hell out of it rather than go to help – that would be merely to commit suicide. I always expected us to be next – I think we just got used to that fear, but it never happened to us.

In March 2003 Dennis told me that Britain and America had invaded Iraq to oust Saddam Hussein. A reporter came to ask me my views. I told him all wars are bad. Ask men who have been to war and they will all tell you the same. Yes, Hussein was an evil man. But the Americans should have toppled him the first time they fought the Iraqis. I felt sorry for soldiers who would once more be risking their lives.

It was not the same as my war. We were fighting for our country and our homes and that is completely different. We had a lot more to lose if we failed. But these troops will not fail. America is too powerful. The US could have done it alone, without our help. The next war will be about food.

On 8 April 2003 I was one of several veterans to meet Prince Charles at the Records Office in Kew, London. The group was led by Jack Davis who was a year older than me.

In 2003 Dennis applied to the French government for Henry's *Légion d'Honneur*, their highest award for outstanding service to France, hoping it would come in time for Henry's 106th birthday. He knew time was pressing. In the space of a month, four veterans he knew well went 'over the top'. Those veterans were Jack Davis, Douglas Thomson, Conrad Leonard and Walter Humphries.

Aged 103, Douglas Thomson was described by one reporter as 'feisty, coherent and charming'. Born in Edinburgh, Thomson lied about his age in order to join up in January 1916. Doing so removed him from an unhappy home life, exonerated him from cross-questioning by street-corner army recruiters and fulfilled his desire to fight for his country. He joined the Honourable Artillery Company, becoming its sole survivor before his death. Thomson trained as a marksman and was duly dispatched to the Somme. The first of his colleagues to die was wearing a suit of body armour provided by his loving mother. However, the victim was shot through the head. Thomson eventually became a runner, carrying messages from headquarters to the front line when the telephones were cut off. Thought to be one of the most dangerous roles of the war, Thomson emerged without a scratch, believing he could calculate where shells were about to land by the noise they made.

In July 2003 I went to the Not Forgotten Association garden party at Buckingham Palace along with eight other veterans. We were all introduced to the Queen, who had special words for everyone. To my delight, David, my eldest grandson, and his wife, Charlotte, also received an invitation. That made the day extra special.

On 21 October I was presented with the *Légion d'Honneur* at the Town Hall in Eastbourne. I arrived in great style, in a white Rolls Royce. The same month I went to the launch of the British Legion Poppy Appeal on HMS *Belfast*.

November meant Armistice Day and only three of us veterans out of a total of 23 were able to attend the national ceremony. Myself, William Stone and Norman Robinson had a combined age of 312 years. For the first time, a vehicle was allowed to join the parade and it was a 92-year-old 15-horsepower Austin open-top tourer recruited to carry us to the Cenotaph. Afterwards, it was lunch at the Grand Plaza Hotel complete with a sing-along of First World War hits.

In December I went with other veterans to the Not Forgotten Association Christmas party. It was held in St James's Palace and we spent plenty of time chatting to royal guest Princess Anne.

Before I knew Dennis well, I always spent Christmas Day with the Rotary Club of Eastbourne. Although the Goodwins offered me a place at their Christmas table, I decided to stick with the Rotary Club. Call it loyalty if you like.

But I always looked forward to spending time with the Goodwins. My routine of spending 12 hours asleep often went out of the window as we sat making conversation or listening to old records. One of my favourites was 'Cigarettes, Whisky and Wild, Wild Women', a very old favourite from the misty past. Around then, I was often asked during interviews how I accounted for living such a long time. Dennis and his wife, Brenda, both suggested I said it was cigarettes, whisky and wild women – so I did and that story stuck with me.

Soon afterwards, I remember visiting Fred Lloyd in his nursing home. There were two women sitting nearby in the lounge and one asked the other, 'Who is that with Fred?'

'It's Henry Allingham,' said the second. 'Don't you remember the television programme about his cigarettes and whisky?'

'Oh yes, and the wild, wild women. Really, at his age. He is even older than Fred.'

In January 2004 a further five First World War veterans passed away. This brought the number remaining to fewer than 30 and, with the death of Henry St John Fancourt, left Henry the sole survivor from the Battle of Jutland. Born in 1900, Henry Fancourt's training at naval college was interrupted by the outbreak of war in 1914 and he was sent to sea in the battle-cruiser Princess Royal, *which was subsequently hit five times during the battle.*

Fancourt was mentioned in dispatches for his conduct on escort duties out of Queenstown (now Cobh), County Cork. In 1919 he saw the German fleet scuttled at Scapa Flow. Five years later he qualified as a pilot and served with the Royal Navy in trouble spots between the wars, including in the Far and Middle East. His service continued during the Second World War. By the time he retired from flying in 1956, he had logged up 1,317 flying hours.

With the 90th anniversary of the start of the First World War in August, 2004 was a big year for remaining veterans like me.

As the date approached, my flat in Eastbourne – and also the Goodwin home nearby where many interviews were conducted – looked more like television studios. My neighbours must have wondered why I was suddenly a celebrity. In the past five years I have been interviewed by television presenters from France, Italy, Holland, Belgium, Argentina, Germany, America, Canada and Russia.

At one event leading up to the anniversary, I was presented with a memento by one of the organisations interested in the First World War. I took it and retired to my wheelchair. But then I was really surprised by Dennis, who took the microphone and said, 'I'm sure you would like Henry to tell you of his experiences.'

He put the microphone into my hands and I was really put on the spot. But there was plenty of applause and that encouraged me to go on. Everyone listened so politely as I spoke about memories from the war. By the time I finished, everyone was standing and clapping. And I liked it. So now it's a case of try stopping me when I get hold of a microphone.

In July that year, a month after I celebrated my 108th birthday, I was given a Veteran's Badge, which was made available to Second World War service people as well as those from the First World War. The ceremony took place in the town hall at Eastbourne and I was presented with the badge alongside Fred Lloyd and William Stone.

Then it was time to mark the outbreak of the First World War. I went to the Cenotaph with Fred Lloyd, William Stone and John Oborne on 4 August. Each veteran chose a part to play. I chose to read the Lord's Prayer.

Afterwards, our wheelchairs were pushed through crowds of clapping and cheering people. At the doors of the Ministry of Defence building, where we were going for lunch, there were hordes of photographers from all over the world. It reminded Fred of his service with the Royal Field Artillery.

John Oborne joined the Devonshire regiment and fought at the Somme. He nearly died when a bullet hit his chest; however, it was deflected by a pocket watch and he lived for a further eight decades. At the 90th anniversary of the outbreak of war, he told Radio 4's Today programme: 'No one would know what it was like unless they were there. Your imagination won't go that far. It is best forgotten. It was that awful.' Just months later, he died in Porthcawl, South Wales, at the age of 104.

While I was at the lunch, an officer from the Royal Air Force asked Dennis if it would be possible for me to go to France, to unveil the British Air Service memorial at St-Omer in September.

The memorial was for all those members of the British Air

Services – the Royal Flying Corps, the Royal Naval Air Services, the Australian Flying Corps, the Royal Air Force and other air forces from the Empire – who served on the Western Front during the First World War. More than 4,000 people from those air services died on the Western Front, of which more than 1,000 have no known grave. The first British aircraft arrived in St-Omer in October 1914 and more than 50 squadrons were based there before the war had finished. I talked it over with Dennis who thought it would be a wonderful opportunity to say thanks for the privileged day I had enjoyed. But I was still reluctant to go back to France.

'You will not be going back to France to relive your experiences,' said Dennis. 'You will be going back personally to represent your fellow comrades at a remembrance service in their honour.'

'Do you think I should go?' I asked, after thinking it over for a few moments.

'Yes.'

'Will you take me?'

'Yes.'

'Then let's go,' I said, and Dennis made the arrangements.

On 10 September an RAF car picked us up from Dennis' house. We enjoyed a good lunch on the way to Folkestone and stayed in a French château before the ceremony at St-Omer. I was given the freedom of St-Omer during an evening concert. Then came the day of the service. It began with a welcome from the mayor of St-Omer and then an introduction by Air Marshal Sir Freddie Sowrey.

Dennis then helped me to the foot of the memorial and handed me the wreath to lay. I stood for a few moments with my head bowed, thinking about the men who had lost their lives. Dennis and I have an understanding – I will manage alone for as long as I can until I put my left hand behind my back, a signal that I now need help to move.

Two months later it was Armistice Day once more and another remembrance parade. In the lead-up to it I was busier than ever before with foreign journalists. One lengthy interview was with the Argentine press, although I have no idea why the people of Argentina would want to know all about me.

On 11 November I went to the memorial service at the Imperial War Museum, where I saw a BC2c aircraft like the one I flew in during the war.

Before the Remembrance Day parade was the British Legion Festival of Remembrance at the Royal Albert Hall. I went with Dennis and met fellow veteran William Stone. We were introduced to the Queen, Prince Philip and Prince Charles. During the performance, the compère Huw Edwards introduced William and me and we were wheeled onto the stage, to thumping applause. It was a wonderful evening – I still can't believe that all this happens to me.

The following morning it was back to the Cenotaph. I began the day with a traditional English breakfast, the best meal of the day, with three cups of tea. We walked the ten minutes it took to get from the Crowne Plaza hotel, in Buckingham Gate, St James, to Horse Guards Parade, and Dennis asked if I could parade with the Fleet Air Arm Association. That created quite a buzz and lots of ex-servicemen shook my hand.

As I was wheeled along the route to the Cenotaph, I was touched by the ripples of spontaneous applause from the crowd. I waved back as much as I could. It was very moving, with so many people in the parade. I'm glad Dennis wrapped me up in blankets, though – I didn't feel the cold. We returned to the Crowne Plaza, which I have come to look on as my London home. The staff and the management are always so kind.

In December I went to Ardingly College in Haywards Heath to talk about details of my life. This occurred after I had originally met them at the Imperial War Museum where they were on a school visit. Dennis and I had talked to them, and Dennis asked if they also taught domestic science as well as history at their school. They said they did, so Dennis then asked if they would bake me a cake? They happily agreed and so we went to see the school, gave a talk on my life, and if you look at the picture section in this book you'll see I received the cake! Dennis researches and organises which venues will best suit me being there to talk about my experiences. The visit started with a concert when pupils played the piano and violin and read poems. They were great.

Then the children asked me questions. One of the questions was: 'What do you think was the greatest invention during your lifetime?'

It was the aeroplane, I told them, as it brings people closer together so that families and friends living across the world can meet. It opens up other countries and helps us to understand each other's way of life.

Later they gave me a Christmas cake, which they had made just for me. They also presented me with flowers, a tie and a booklet of poems and letters that I had inspired. We all had lunch together. The teacher told Dennis afterwards that the children were still talking about the visit days later.

Soon afterwards it was the Not Forgotten Association Christmas party and I met Prince Charles for the third time – we had spoken at the Records Office in Kew in April 2003 and at the British Legion Festival of Remembrance at the Royal Albert Hall in November.

With the turn of 2005 there were twenty known First World War veterans in Britain, three in Australia and one in Canada. Almost immediately there was bad news. Charles Watson, a member of the Royal Flying Corps, died on New Year's Day. Dennis had been planning to take me to meet him in the spring but it was not to be. The same month, Charles Hardy died in a nursing home in Porthcawl, South Wales, and later in the year, my friend Fred Lloyd passed away.

Born in Hampshire in 1899, Charles Watson volunteered for the Royal Flying Corps at the age of 18, as soon as he left school. He did so despite warnings from his father, who was fighting in France with the Somerset Light Infantry, that planes were regularly being shot down. By the spring of 1918, Charles was dispatched to No. 11 Squadron in France as an observer. In August his plane was attacked during a bombing mission on the Western Front and his pilot temporarily blinded by smoke. Using a detachable joystick, Watson nosedived into cloud-cover and then executed an almost perfect landing close to the French lines. He then dragged the pilot to safety, with both men making it back to Allied territory in safety.

Charles Hardy, a non-combatant, was the last known survivor of the Enniskillen Dragoons.

Born in 1898, Fred Lloyd had already lost a brother in the Battle of the Somme and nearly died himself before serving in France. Having joined the Royal Artillery, he contracted meningitis and was thought by doctors lucky to be alive when he survived. He had already been turned down by his local Sussex regiment for being too small. Fred ended up in the Army Veterinary Corps. One of 16 children, he ultimately lost two brothers to the war. Afterwards, he became a gardener and retired in 1968, aged 70 – the year Harold Wilson became Prime Minister. Later, Lloyd summed up the dichotomy facing veterans like himself to the Guardian *newspaper when he said: 'War is not a wonderful thing to be remembered but those who died must never be forgotten.'*

For the first time in 2005 I experienced a car boot sale. It was just a load of junk on sale but people were buying it. Someone recognised me from the television coverage and came to shake my hand. A stall holder remarked that I must be an antique. 'Wheel him over here and I will see how much I can get for him.'

In March I returned to Great Yarmouth, where I had started service and met Dorothy all those years ago – it was very emotional. I found the road where I had been billeted and had had lunch with the Cater family.

Soon afterwards I went to the Tangmere Military Aviation Museum near Chichester. While I was there, I met Neville Duke, a Second World War ace with 28 'kills' who broke the world speed record, and Battle of Britain pilot Nick Berryman. Curiously, Duke was a friend of Donald Campbell, with whom I had worked at the beginning of the war.

During April and May the lift at my flat was broken. It meant negotiating three flights of stairs, slowly and with Dennis' help. One day, as I waited at the bottom for Dennis to bring down my wheelchair, Dennis fell down a flight of stairs, landing with the chair on top of him. I wondered what had kept him so long.

In November came news of the death of Alfred Anderson, the last of the *Old Contemptibles* – these were British fighters who proudly bore the name, supposedly after the Kaiser called the forces assembling in France 'a contemptible little army'.

'I'll give Christmas Day 1914 a brief thought, as I do every year. And I'll think about all my friends who never made it home. But it's too sad to think too much about it. Far too sad.'

That was the response of veteran Alfred Anderson to the barrage of questions about the famous Christmas Day truce of 1914. The war, although only a few months old, had been waged in earnest. But on

Christmas morning, Allied soldiers on the Western Front were transfixed by the sound of their German counterparts singing carols: 'Stille Nacht, heilige Nacht.' If the words were unfamiliar, the tune was not and soon the British added their voices to the rendition of 'Silent Night'. Then a lone German infantryman popped up, holding a small tree glowing with light. 'Merry Christmas. We not shoot, you not shoot.'

At first, Allied soldiers were hesitant. Could it be a trick to lure them into dangerous exposed territory? But soon they went into No Man's Land to greet German soldiers coming in the opposite direction. They shook hands, sang, smoked and swapped tunic buttons. They even played football, using empty bully beef cans as a ball.

British officers remained aloof as the unauthorised truce swept across much of the 500-mile Western Front. But they did not try to tempt soldiers back from this unorthodox and impromptu camaraderie.

Alfred Anderson was spending that cold Christmas at a derelict farmhouse slightly behind the lines. Born in 1896, the same year as Henry, in Alyth, Perthshire, Anderson had been a member of the Territorial Army since the age of 16 and had joined the Black Watch with many of his friends at the outbreak of war. The unaccustomed silence that Christmas morning alerted Anderson and his fellow soldiers that something was amiss. Until then, the artillery barrage accompanied by the rattle of machine guns had continued around the clock.

Alfred Anderson fought at Mons, Neuve Chapelle and Loos. At one stage he was batman to Captain Fergus Bowes-Lyon, the brother of the Queen Mother, who died in 1915, while her death aged 101 was in 2002.

As a part-time undertaker at home, Anderson was well used to the sight of dead bodies. Nonetheless, he was devastated by the death of a succession of friends. Once, during a visit home, he was barred from the house of a dead chum, where he had gone to pay his respects. When he asked why, the soldier's grieving sisters told him: 'Because you're here and he's not.'

In 1916 Alfred received serious shrapnel injuries to the neck and shoulder. He was invalided home, where he became a staff sergeant in a training camp in Yorkshire. There he met and married Susanna, and the couple returned to Alfred's Scottish home town to take over his father's joinery business. They celebrated a diamond wedding anniversary before Susanna's death aged 83.

At his death in November 2005, aged 109, Alfred Anderson was the oldest man in Scotland and the last known holder of the Mons Star. He was survived by four children – having helped one to celebrate a golden wedding anniversary before his death – ten grandchildren, eighteen great-grandchildren and two great-great-grandchildren.

At the beginning of 2006 there were 11 known survivors in Britain. The talk in the papers was about how to mark the passing of the last one.

'Don't think that I will be the last to go,' I told journalists. 'I am ready now.'

Years ago I had decided to leave my body to science. I did this because of my association with hospitals during the Second World War. I also thought it would save anyone the trouble of arranging my funeral. I wasn't sure who would want to go to it, anyway. But Dennis wasn't sure I had done the right thing.

'Everything is different now,' he explained. 'You have achieved celebrity status. Every event you attend attracts the media which in turn arouses the interest of the public at large.

'Remember, I am always standing just behind you on these occasions. I see not only the transformation in you but the profound effect you have on people. People of my generation see in you their fathers and grandfathers. They admire the way you display your courage and strength and sensitivities, keeping alive the memory of our forefathers who made the ultimate sacrifice.

I'm sure they will want to mourn your death just as they mourn their own family.

'When you die, I think there will be a surge of emotion tinged with patriotism. I firmly believe you owe it to those people to have a funeral at which they can mourn your passing – and that of others in your generation.'

Overnight I thought about what Dennis said. I realised he was probably right. My role now is to remind people of the sacrifices made in the First World War and that needs to go on as long as possible. So I agreed to a funeral and cremation.

I couldn't speak for the other veterans except to say that, deep down, most people would like to go out in style, especially those with strong military connections. Drums, bugles and banners can tell you a lot about the man they are heralding.

Dennis was asked to contribute to the debate by Don Touhig, the defence minister responsible for veterans. Grief is personal, Dennis told him, but at the considerable number of veterans' funerals that he had attended in the past 20 years, there was often a military presence. But he doubted any of the families would want to be at the centre of a media circus. On 14 July 2006 he received this letter from MP Tom Watson.

> We are all very conscious that the few remaining World War I veterans are now very old and the death of the last one will be widely recognised as of major national importance. The profile of the event to mark it must reflect this. A State funeral would not be appropriate as it would be wrong to single out one individual as this was a sacrifice made by a whole generation. The last veteran would not be an 'unknown warrior' but an identifiable individual who would be subject to media scrutiny. Reinforcing this, you advised that a number of surviving veterans and

their families have already indicated that they would not welcome the intrusion that would come with being singled out in this way and these views should be respected.

It is the intention, therefore, to mark the death of the last known WWI veteran with a national memorial service for the whole of that generation. This would include not only the contribution of the UK Armed Forces but also that of the civilian population and the role of the Empire in the war.

I am sure that you will be pleased to know that Her Majesty is supportive of a national memorial service and that the Royal British Legion and the Confederation of British Service and Ex-Service Organisations also back the proposal.

. . . [I]n essence the memorial service will be held in Westminster Abbey within about 12 weeks of the death of the last known veteran (unless timing allows for the event to coincide with the weekend of Remembrance Sunday).

The service will be preceded by a ceremonial procession involving an empty gun carriage that will deliberately replicate some of the sombre pageantry associated with the burial of the Unknown Warrior some 86 years ago.

In order to ensure that as many people as possible have the opportunity to be a part of this significant event, an educational resource pack will be distributed to primary and secondary schools following the death of the last veteran.

In the early months of 2006, Dennis noticed that Henry's health was deteriorating. The month of January somehow manages to find a chink in the armour of the elderly and Henry was displaying signs that he was physically below par. He was eating less, wheezing more and often dozed off when previously he had been alert for long periods.

Henry blamed the weather for his ills. He told Dennis that he knew best what his body needed, which was rest, castor oil and a careful diet. In a few weeks, he promised, he would be as good as new.

And his health did improve, until, a few weeks later, he fell and cracked his head, needing hospital treatment. Afterwards, the hospital released him into the care of St Dunstan's, a specialist centre for blind ex-servicemen and -women in Ovingdean, Sussex. Henry had been certified blind a few months previously following an extensive eye examination.

However, Henry was resolutely against giving up his flat in favour of a home – he knew he had the full support and love of the Goodwins to fall back on. Fifteen years earlier, he had booked himself into a nursing home following an operation. He never spoke about his experiences there, other than to say they were the worst few days he had had in all his life. He vowed never to live in a home, despite visiting many other veterans living happily in excellent residential and care homes. 'Don't you ever put me in one of those places,' he urged Dennis.

At the end of March, Henry once again collapsed, went to hospital and was dispatched to St Dunstan's. Dennis implored him to think again about his future. 'You are not fit enough to return to your flat,' he told him. 'Why not give it a try?'

Only after a sustained campaign did Dennis win the battle, as Henry agreed to live at St Dunstan's.

On 21 April I became a freeman of Eastbourne. Getting the freedom of the borough is about the highest honour any town or city can give someone. It was one of my proudest moments. I hadn't been born in Eastbourne but had lived there for 42 years and I loved it.

Just two weeks later, I was on my way to the Oval, the home of Surrey cricket, where I had last visited 103 years previously.

That was when I saw W.G. Grace playing for Gloucestershire. I remembered the games I had had as a youngster, using a gas lamp standard as a wicket. We never came off for bad light. Mind you, we always had to have a third man. It was his job to keep an eye out for approaching policemen. It was an offence to play cricket in the street and you could be fined. I can remember a few games being called off – Bobby stopped play.

I was allowed to go onto the turf at the Oval, thanks to the groundsman. With my eyesight nearly gone, I rely a lot on my sense of touch and I ran my hands backwards and forwards across the manicured grass. As I straightened up and faced the field, where the game was in progress, Gloucester's last wicket fell, giving victory to Surrey. As they left the field, I met the Surrey players, including captain Mark Butcher. There was applause from the crowd as I disappeared into the pavilion, 109 not out.

While I was there, I was interviewed by Sky TV for a programme, called *Shot at Dawn*, about the young soldiers executed for cowardice during the First World War – this debate had been raging for some years now. I pointed out that it was alleged cowardice. It is this issue that has been questioned. Those men had gone willingly into battle, many of them as volunteers like me, and were prepared to face death. Who knows how they felt and what effect the chaos, turmoil, disorientation and confusion of trench warfare had on their senses? The guilty verdict might have been sound 90 years ago but, by today's standards, there's an element of doubt. It was right that pardons were issued.

In 2006 Defence Secretary Des Browne announced that more than 300 British soldiers shot during the First World War for cowardice and desertion would be pardoned.

Private Bernard McGeehan, of the Liverpool King's Regiment, is perhaps a typical example of those who were executed. He was killed by firing squad on 2 November 1916 after being found guilty of desertion. Aged 28 and from Derry, Northern Ireland, he had been transferred to the front line just after the Battle of the Somme earlier that year. Shell-shocked, shaking and lost, he walked away from his lines, obviously contravening military codes. However, five days later he wandered back, still in a bewildered state but belying the contention that he planned to escape.

The announcement of the pardon came after years of campaigning from the family of Private Harry Farr. His daughter Gertrude Harris, who was three years old at the time of his death, told the BBC: 'I am so relieved that this ordeal is now over and I can be content knowing that my father's memory is intact.

'I have always argued that my father's refusal to rejoin the front line, described in the court martial as resulting from cowardice, was in fact the result of shellshock, and I believe that many other soldiers suffered from this, not just my father.'

Pte Farr was one of Kitchener's earliest volunteers. He had already served in the British Army between 1908 and 1912. But in 1914 he gave up his job as a London scaffolder and kissed goodbye to his wife and daughter, both called Gertrude.

He fought at the first Battle of the Somme and at Neuve Chapelle but during 1915 and 1916 his nerves deteriorated. He reported sick four times, once spending five months in hospital with what his family believes to have been shellshock.

Nonetheless, he went back to the front line with the West Yorkshire Regiment, but was court martialled after refusing to go to the trenches in September 1916, saying he could no longer stand the thud of the artillery.

At his court martial on 16 October 1916, Pte Farr was found guilty of 'misbehaving before the enemy in such a manner as to show cowardice'. He was shot the following morning, aged 25, having refused a blindfold so that he could look the soldiers of the firing squad squarely in the eye.

THE OLDEST WARRIOR
Henry visiting RAF Cosford, sits in front of the plane he is most associated with –
the BE2c – in which he saw a great deal of active service on the Western Front.

A MAN AND HIS MEMORIES
Henry takes great pride in representing the
very last survivors of the Great War. He attends
a variety of remembrance services with the aid
of the World War One Veterans Association.

LOVE IN WAR
Henry was fortunate enough in 2006 to meet
Germany's oldest surviving Great War veteran
– Robert Mair – and both men were moved to
tears to embrace and state all was forgiven.

MEETING THE MASTER
Henry's past catches up with him as
he sees a bust of W G Grace at Lords
– did he resemble the living legend he
witnessed playing all those years ago?

MEETING ROYALTY
Henry greets HRH Prince
Charles. Both Henry
and Dennis wear their
respective Great War and
Second World War medals.

MEETING THE NEW GENERATION
Whilst on his pilgrimage to the RAF memorial at
St Omer in France, Henry greets the latest batch of
recruits from RAF Cosford in November 2005.

PASSING ON THE MESSAGE

With the help of Dennis Goodwin – centre of picture – Henry is able to meet and talk to a wide variety of people, such as Air Vice Marshal Peter Dye of the RAF, who has been a great supporter over the years.

MEETING THE GREAT AND THE GOOD

Henry enjoys telling his story – whether it be the incumbent Prime Minister Gordon Brown . . .

. . . or, with meeting the thousands of school children he has encountered during his many educational trips with the World War One Veterans Association.

ORIGINAL RAF MEETS
THE NEW BATCH
Henry shares a joke with
new recruits from RAF
Cosford in 2005.

HAPPY CHRISTMAS
Henry, together with
Brenda and Dennis
Goodwin of the World
War One Veterans
Association, receives
a christmas cake from
young school children
who are ever eager to
hear about the life of
Britain's oldest veteran.

A PILOT AT LAST!
Sharing a joke with crews
from RAF Cosford as Henry
wears a World War Two
airman's head gear.

THE WARHORSE
The BE2c – seen restored here at an air show – was the plane flown by the majority of RNAS squadrons during the Great War. It was used for bombing, reconnaissance and anti-submarine flights.

PALS TOGETHER
Henry stands shoulder to shoulder with his friend and confidante Dennis Goodwin. It is with him he has attended many veterans commemorations, such as this one at St Omer in France.

TWO LIVING LEGENDS
Dame Vera Lynn – 'The Forces Sweetheart' – happily greets and talks to Henry at a veterans day get together. Henry would have been 21 years old when Dame Lynn was born in 1917.

A CARD FROM THE QUEEN
Since he turned 100 years old, Henry annually receives a birthday card from Her Majesty the Queen, and he treasures every one.

THE LAST VETERANS

Henry poses outside a reception at Ten Downing Street with Harry Patch – sitting at left (110 years old) – and William 'Bill' Stone – standing behind (107 years of age). Their combined ages are a staggering 329 years.

A PROMISED KEPT

Vice Admiral Adrian Johns (pictured standing far left) had promised Henry on his 110th birthday that the following year he would have it on HMS *Victory*. True to his word, that is where it was hosted, in attendance with many of his friends such as Brenda and Dennis Goodwin, and family from the USA – his grandson David Gray kneels on the right of Henry's wheelchair.

THE PRIDE OF OUR COUNTRY

Henry receives a unique honour – receiving 'The Pride of Britain Award' at the *Daily Mirror*'s televised event from Dame Vera Lynn and surrounded by all his grandchildren and great-grandchildren.

THE LAST VOLUNTEER

Looking out on his beloved beach at Eastbourne, Henry ponders the incredible life he has lived and those who died in order that he might enjoy it.

HAPPY BIRTHDAY HENRY!
Henry, together with Peter Dye and Dennis and Brenda Goodwin watch
the RAF fly past to celebrate his 112th birthday on 6 June 2008.
(© David Gray)

An army chaplain at the execution sent Pte Farr's widow a message saying 'a finer soldier never lived'. Pte Farr was not the first to be shot. That accolade goes to Private Thomas Highgate, of the Royal West Kent Regiment, who was shot for desertion just 35 days into the conflict. Remarkably, his offence, trial, sentencing and execution all took place on the same day – 8 September 1914.

Aged just 17, he was tortured by the terrors of the Battle of Mons and sought shelter in a barn. Pte Highgate was undefended at his court martial because all his regimental comrades were dead, injured or had been taken prisoners of war. His case draws into sharp focus the controversy the issue still causes, as 86 years later, in 2000, the parish council of Shoreham, Kent, where Pte Highgate lived, voted not to include his name on its war memorial.

Phil Hobson, who was council chairman at the time, said: 'We had the opportunity of putting his name on it because we were replacing the plaque with all the names on – after nearly 100 years it was very worn. We took what we thought to be the best compromise position in that a space was left for his name should people want it to be added at a later date.'

Even younger was Private Herbert Burden, who at 16 lied so that he could join the Northumberland Fusiliers and fight in the war. When he was led out before the firing squad on 21 July 1915, he was still just 17 – still officially 'too young' to be in the regiment.

Pte Burden had been court-martialled for desertion after ten months' service. He had left his post to comfort a recently bereaved friend stationed nearby. He himself had seen many comrades slaughtered.

It was Pte Burden's case that led John Hipkin, a retired Newcastle teacher, to set up the Shot at Dawn campaign in the early 1990s. A memorial to soldiers shot by their own side during the First World War was unveiled in Staffordshire in 2001. The statue of a young soldier blindfolded and tied to a stake was modelled on Pte Burden.

The village of Furstow in Lincolnshire did not have a war memorial for the seven local men who died during the First World War until 2005. That's because one of the number was shot at dawn and public opinion was divided about whether or not he should be included among the celebrated. Private Kirman of the Lincolnshire Regiment was injured at Mons and the Somme, two notorious killing grounds. Aged 32 when he was shot on 23 September 1917, he had been in the Army for nine years prior to the outbreak of war.

Pte Kirman was injured several times and sent home to recuperate but, in September 1917, he felt he could not take any more and went absent without leave. After two days, he handed himself in to the military police, was court martialled and shot at dawn.

When some local people objected to his inclusion on the war memorial, others, who had lost sons and husbands, subsequently refused to allow the use of their loved ones' names.

Nicola Pike, who successfully campaigned for a memorial including his name, said: 'There would have been somebody in the village who disagreed with it, so the rest of the families said, "If you're not having him, then you're not having our boys, because they all went to school together and worked together."'

The route to universal pardons has been fraught with difficulties. Five successive British governments have refused to bend on the issue. There has been a reluctance to second-guess those who dispensed justice at the time. Given that each case was different, ministers have veered away from the concept of a blanket pardon. There were, it has been pointed out, at least 80,000 cases of shellshock recorded in the First World War but only a relatively small number resulted in charges of cowardice or desertion.

Nor have all veterans been in favour of universal pardons. Albert 'Smiler' Marshall maintained that military justice was both necessary and effective.

Born in 1897, Smiler joined the Essex Yeomanry and was, before his death in 2005 aged 108, the last man alive who fought on horseback, wielding a sword, for the British Army. Although his mother died when he was four years old, he had a happy childhood caring for farmyard animals as well as ponies and horses, which he rode from the age of five.

At 13, he left school to work as an apprentice shipwright. However, when Lord Kitchener visited Colchester as part of his 1914 recruitment drive, Albert decided to sign up. An army officer asked his date of birth and he replied truthfully. Since at 17 he was officially too young to be in the Army, the army officer asked him to 'go outside and think again'. Moments later, the young man entered the office again, as if he'd never been before, and gave his birth date as 1896.

One day, during a winter's day exercise session, he surreptitiously lobbed a snowball at the man in front. When the drill sergeant bellowed at him, he looked the picture of innocence. However, the sergeant wasn't fooled. 'Yes, son, I'm talking to you, Smiler.' The name stuck.

After being sent to France in 1915, he was gassed twice, then, in the Battle of Loos, his trigger finger was blown off. Perhaps worse still, his best friend was shot beside him as they stood in a trench. Smiler never forgot that his friend's mother received her dead son's pay-packet minus one pound, the cost of the blanket in which he was buried. Smiler could have been invalided out of the army. Instead, he re-mustered in the machine-gun corps.

Speaking at the age of 105, Smiler related his wartime experiences to the Guardian *and* Observer *newspapers. Recalling an incident in 1917, he said:*

> One afternoon at about 4 p.m. we learned that soldiers from
> the Oxford and Bucks regiment were to go over the top at
> 6 p.m. By nine o'clock every single one of them was dead.

We went out with the Royal Army Medical Corps to bury them all. An officer held up a white stick as we went into No Man's Land. It was a sign to ask the enemy to stop firing, and they did. We could only dig down a few feet and cover them with a bit of soil, burying them where they lay. It was horrible. By the next day, there was nothing – just plain ground again. Yet underneath, just a foot deep, was all that battalion. All dead.

However, despite the appalling horrors faced by soldiers and the shocking waste of life, Smiler still felt it would be wrong to issue pardons for those shot at dawn.

I didn't know anyone who was executed or who had anything to do with a firing squad, but we all knew about the penalty. But it didn't occur to you not to fight. You didn't think about it, you just did it. And you just took what came your way. You lived in these trenches for days and days with nothing happening but bombardments. You regularly lost a friend or someone near you. The thought never left you that you could be next.

Smiler saw at first hand the brutality of military punishment:

One day I was ordered to stand guard over a chap who had been tied to a wheel, without food or water, as a punishment for something. I can't remember what he'd done. But I felt sorry for him so I put my fag up to his lips so he could have a smoke. It was a very risky thing to do because if anyone had seen me they'd have tied me to the wheel as well!

Years later, I was walking down Oxford Street in London
and I saw him. He recognised me immediately and thanked
me. He said he'd never forgotten that fag.

*After the First World War ended, Smiler served in Ireland and
eventually returned to England in 1921 to marry his childhood
sweetheart, Florence, and find a job on an estate. At the age of 85 he
was still competing on horseback. Aged 100, he held down a job in a
greenhouse. When he died, he had outlived four of his five children.*

*Fellow veteran Jack Davis, one of Kitchener's volunteers, saw all
sides of the issue while serving in the army. He went AWOL and
risked being shot; he was almost selected for firing squad duty; and
he saw men suffering from shellshock. The story of his war is unlike
most others.*

*Jack believed that his two brothers, William and Percy, had been
rejected from the Army. But one dark night he approached a trench
ahead of his comrades and received the usual challenge of 'Halt, who
goes there?'*

*Instantly, he recognised the voice of his older brother, Percy, and
discovered that William was not far away – both standing thigh-deep
in trench water.*

*'It was indescribable, the emotions,' Jack said. 'But I had a job to do
so it was just a few words, then "see you".'*

*Later, he heard his brothers' brigade had taken numerous casualties.
He instantly made the potentially fatal decision of going to find them,
to ensure they were still alive. Keeping off the roads, he went to the area
they were in and found Percy alive and well. William, he learned, was
being treated for wounds.*

*'When I returned to my brigade I was immediately arrested. I was
given the choice between a court martial or my commanding officer's
punishment. I took his punishment and lost three days' pay. Had I got
lost on my way back to my unit and been caught by soldiers who didn't*

know me, who would have believed my story? I'd have been shot.'

He was almost detailed for a firing squad, but missed out at the last minute. Jack knew that if he had been given the task, he would have carried it out, but felt a great sense of relief after the eventual outcome.

Jack never panicked, even in the face of danger. He maintained the conviction that he was going to stay alive, despite the carnage all around him.

'Keeping a clear head wasn't easy and many men cracked,' he said. 'I was once sent out with another man into No Man's Land to a shell crater by the German trench. They were just yards away – you could hear them talking and stamping their feet to keep warm. Unfortunately, my comrade was shellshocked. He was whimpering like a child.'

Jack abandoned the mission and returned his partner to the safety of the Allied line from where he was dispatched for treatment. Said Jack, 'I have thought a lot about the 306 men who were executed for cowardice or desertion. I think most were either shellshocked or not calm in the mind.'

Above the loss of those men, Jack questioned whether the gains from that war – or any other – were worth the supreme sacrifice by so many young men. 'I would not agree to participate in any form of warfare again. Wars have proved nothing, other than that everyone emerges from them as a loser in some way or another.'

The weekend after my trip to the Oval, Dennis, Brenda and I stood outside a local supermarket rattling tins in aid of a forces' charity. My tin was soon heavier than either of the others.

In 2006 I was nominated for an award in the public life category of the Morgan Stanley 'Great Britons' award. I went to the presentation where Al Gore, the former US vice president and green campaigner, was speaking. I didn't win the award but while I was at the reception at the Guildhall, in the City of London, I stopped in front of a huge painting, probably 6 ft by 6 ft, of Queen Victoria's diamond jubilee.

'I believe my grandfather took me to the City of London to see that,' I told Dennis. 'We stood near the Stock Exchange, or so I was told. Can you see a small boy on the shoulders of a tall man?'

Dennis scrutinised the picture but he couldn't see anyone who matched that description. As I pointed out, we must have been standing further along the road. I was just a year old at the time.

I was being filmed for a documentary called *Henry's War*. For that I visited the Shuttleworth Collection at Biggleswade, Bedfordshire, where there's a collection of First World War aircraft. Although most are replicas, there is an original Bristol fighter. I went around the museum, touching rather than looking at the planes.

Outside I saw the original Bristol and a Sopwith triplane replica take off, and I chatted to the mechanics about how they should be serviced. Before they landed, they took a low-level flight over my head. As Dennis put it, it was another close encounter with my past.

I visited St Andrew's School in Eastbourne in May. My flat overlooked the playing fields so I felt I had got to know the pupils over the years. For the first time, though, I looked around the school and met pupils and teachers face-to-face. I had lunch there – I wish I'd had meals like that one in front of me when I was their age. I was brought up to respect meals served to me and not throw any away. If I left anything on my plate, there was the danger that the next plate wouldn't be so full. Often I sing a little when I'm visiting children.

Henry's world is almost completely noiseless. If he sings, he can hear his voice, he is physically doing something and he knows he is alive. Often when he is silent you think he is nodding off. Then, for some unknown

reason, he will suddenly break into a song. Dennis is sure Henry sings
to reassure himself that everything is all right.

At the end of the month, I took part in an exhibition to mark
the 90th anniversary of the Battle of Jutland. The ceremony took
place on HMS *Belfast* and was officially opened by the Duchess
of Gloucester (our association's patron). When she spoke to the
audience, the Duchess, originally from Denmark, told how the
battle could be heard in her home country, some 30 miles inland.
Danish people buried the bodies of both British and German
sailors washed up on their shores.

I celebrated my 110th birthday at the Grand Hotel in Eastbourne.
Dennis and Brenda had organised eveything. My family was
there – grandsons David, Paul, Timothy and Christopher, along
with two great-grandchildren and two great-great-grandchildren.
The great-grandchildren were David's son Nathaniel, there with
his wife, Jana, and David's daughter Amy, accompanied by her
husband, Chris, and their two children, Lauren, almost two, and
six-week-old Eric.

In the morning Gordon Brown, then the Chancellor of the
Exchequer, and Des Browne, Defence Secretary, presented me with
the Queen's birthday card. It read: 'I send my warm congratulations
on the celebration of your 110th birthday on 6 June 2006. May
your celebration be particularly happy and memorable.' There was
a handwritten letter from Prince Charles and one from Sir Jock
Stirrup, Chief of the Defence Staff.

Eastbourne MP Nigel Waterson tabled a motion in the House of
Commons congratulating Henry on his special day. It read: 'This
House congratulates Eastbourne resident Mr Henry Allingham on his
110th birthday; marks with respect his long years of active service on
the Western Front and in the Battle of Jutland during the First World

War; considers him a splendid example of the courage, devotion to service and humility of his generation; and wishes him many more happy years.'

Along with the Queen's birthday card, the Chancellor presented Henry with a copy of the budget statement delivered in 1896 and joked, 'I think the price of whisky was a bit lower then.' Other dignitaries celebrating with Henry included Vice-Admiral Adrian Johns, Second Sea Lord of the Fleet Air Arm; Air Vice-Marshal Peter Dye; and Peter Field, Vice-Lord Lieutenant for East Sussex. But the best was still to come. At midday, two Tornados from No. 31 Squadron and a Naval Sea Hawk, from the Royal Navy Historic Flight (RNHF), passed over the hotel by way of salute.

My cake was rectangular, inscribed with the words 'Dear Henry, Happy 110th Birthday' and had 11 candles, one for each decade. David helped me cut the cake, which was then passed around among the guests.

Before he left, Admiral Johns told me he would be happy to host the next birthday celebrations aboard HMS *Victory* in Portsmouth. It was, said Dennis, a good reason for living, especially as he could take a back seat in the arrangements on that occasion.

twelve

EDUCATING FUTURE GENERATIONS

AFTER THE CLIMAX OF Henry's 110th birthday party, Dennis made sure that Henry stayed active and busy so he wouldn't come down to earth with a bump. Having looked after veterans for the last 20 years, he realises the importance of trying to coax out of them the desire and willingness to accept that tomorrow is the beginning of the rest of their lives.

Those chronological years need not necessarily blunt their zest for life. The ravages of the ageing process can often be overcome. In the early days of the World War One Veterans' Association, veterans were promised that if they were willing to travel, Dennis would get them to where they wanted to go. It is a promise that remains unbroken today. He carefully planned for Henry events which were not too taxing but nonetheless challenging. One of them was a visit to RAF Cosford in Staffordshire.

Henry not only enjoys the company of servicemen and -women, but their way of life animates him. Henry has long since told me that he spends most of his time tuned in to his memories, His resurrection, as he calls it, now involves him relating his experiences. Most people he talks to want to know about life during the 1914–18 war. Henry retreats into this period of his life and also remembers the everyday life of a serviceman outside the war. He recalls with fondness his time in the mess, talking across the table to fellow ratings. He told Dennis: 'Somehow you feel safe and secure.'

At the Defence College of Aeronautical Engineering in Cosford, we were greeted by RAF personnel. My job this time was to officially open a new wing for the Survival Equipment Training School, along with Air Vice-Marshal Peter Dye. We had a tour of the building and it was fascinating to see the survival equipment available to the men and women who guard our skies. With new technology and advances in man-made fibres, the equipment provides greater strength and safety than ever before. I kept wishing we'd had this kind of equipment in my day. I couldn't help but think of the pilot who bled to death because no one knew how to apply a simple tourniquet. Think of how many others could have been saved with these new advances.

In my day, aircraft survival equipment was limited to the plough rope I used to secure Little Woods when he did the loop the loop. I wonder, was I the first survival equipment fitter?

Whenever I go to a military establishment, I always make a point of congratulating servicemen and -women on their choice of profession. If I had my time over again, I wouldn't mind having another go.

When Dennis told me that men and women in uniform were being abused in the street, I was dismayed. The misguided individuals hurling abuse were blaming the servicemen and women for the wars in Iraq and Afghanistan. What is the country coming to? These young men and women in the services should wear their uniform with pride and discipline. Ignore this loutish behaviour. And next time you see men and women in uniform, ask if you can shake their hand. Tell them that we are proud of what they do, because they are doing it for you and me.

The next day I went to the RAF Museum at Cosford, where I encountered a group of excitable youngsters and I spoke to them about my wartime experiences.

On 20 June I joined the London Taxi Benevolent Association for War Disabled on its annual outing to Worthing, a day devoted to disabled veterans. The Benevolent Association has been good to me and I could not possibly have fulfilled my engagements in London without it.

Following a request from the taxi drivers, Dennis asked if the Duchess of Gloucester would attend. She did so, even though it was her 60th birthday. I gave her a card, signed by myself and the other two surviving First World War veterans.

If that wasn't enough, Dennis, Brenda and I also went to Veteran's Day at the Imperial War Museum, followed by a visit to 10 Downing Street, to meet Prime Minister Tony Blair, his wife, Cherie, Deputy Prime Minister John Prescott and Chancellor Gordon Brown. Gordon Brown approached me immediately, reminding me it was only three weeks since we had seen one another at my birthday.

To mark the 90th anniversary of the Battle of the Somme, I went to France with Dennis and Brenda. Thirteen divisions of Kitchener's army set off under the umbrella of artillery barrage on 1 July 1916. At the end of the first day of battle, 60,000 men had fallen, of which over 19,000 were dead. Never before had Britain and her empire suffered such a catastrophe. It was a black day for the British Army. During the stalemate that followed, there were 3,000 casualties a day.

Soon after arriving at the hotel in La Touquet, Henry told Dennis he would like to go to bed.

'I got up far too early this morning,' he said. 'I've eaten enough for one day. I'll turn in. Off you go and get your supper. I'll be all right. You know the drill – you'll be back in time to settle me down for the night.'

Dennis, Brenda and the RAF officers on the trip found a fish restaurant and soaked up the atmosphere, as France were playing that night in a World Cup football match.

Shortly after 11 p.m., the group returned to the hotel and Dennis went to check on Henry. He found Henry on the bed, close to the edge, and decided to move him over slightly.

'How was it, boy?' Henry piped up.

He then announced that he was hungry and wanted a glass of cola and some ice cream. At nearly 11.30 p.m., Dennis reluctantly made his way downstairs, wondering how to frame the unusual request. Fortunately, the receptionist understood and assured him it was no problem.

When Henry had polished off the drink and ice cream, he went back to sleep immediately.

We visited St-Omer while we were in France. I was interviewed at the air station by the BBC and we had lunch there before motoring to another aerodrome, at Thiepval. Replicas of a Sopwith triplane and an SE5 stood on the runway, ready for a fly-past planned for the following day. When Dennis wheeled me up to the first aircraft, I held out my hand and immediately identified it as a Sopwith, just by touch. I gave another interview, carried out in the blazing sunshine.

That night I'd decided on fish and chips for my dinner. We went back to the restaurant Dennis and Brenda had visited the evening before – but there was bad news. The restaurant didn't sell chips.

Yet when he found out who we were, the proprietor served the fish and bought chips from across the road to complete the meal.

The Memorial to the Missing of the Somme at Thiepval honours the 72,085 Commonwealth Soldiers who died during the Battle of the Somme. The memorial was designed by Sir Edwin Lutyens, stands 150 ft high and is perched impressively on a ridge overlooking the battlefields. It was unveiled by Edward, Prince of Wales (later King Edward VIII), on 31 July 1932.

Dennis had previously brought some 20 veterans to the ceremony that marked the 80th anniversary of the battle, in 1996. It was nearly the death of him getting the men back up to the Front all those years later wheeling them all across such uneven terrain.

This time, in 2006, it was a relatively short walk. And as he wheeled Henry along the path, people stood and cheered. The further they went, the more the cheering intensified. It was emotionally draining for both Henry and Dennis. People used Henry's appearance as a means to show their compassion for those involved in the event that had taken place 90 years ago.

During the sun-drenched ceremony, Henry renewed his acquaintance with Prince Charles and the Duke and Duchess of Gloucester. Dennis made several attempts to wheel him away from the service into the shade, but the veteran refused, saying, 'I'm fine – sitting pretty.'

Afterwards, they went to the hospitality tent for water and fresh fruit to revive the old soldier, who had eventually flagged in the heat.

Meanwhile, Brenda had gone outside to inspect a smart Bentley that had drawn up. It was Prince Charles' vehicle and, before he and Camilla got inside, they approached Brenda to ask if Henry was all right, given the intense heat. Henry was well, she told them, and already back in harness, talking to French and Belgian TV stations after a short spell of recuperation.

Soon after we got back from France, Dennis took a telephone call from actress Nicola McAuliffe, who had read about me in the newspapers. She was appearing in a Noel Coward play at the Devonshire Park Theatre in Eastbourne and invited me to a performance. I was all for it as I'd been to the theatre a number of times in the past. I could barely see or hear the play and Noel Coward was not really my cup of tea, but it did trigger some memories. I never thought I would go to the theatre again. Now Dennis and Nicola had together made the impossible possible. Afterwards, I was introduced to the cast. I treated them to some stories, jokes and songs from Victorian and Edwardian theatre.

I went to a garden party in Admiralty House, Portsmouth, where Admiral Jolns invited me to take the salute. This was hotly followed by the Buckingham Palace Garden Party, held each year in July by the Not Forgotten Association. Then there was a special treat at St Dunstan's when Nicola McAuliffe organised a concert with three others. It ended with a sing-along of wartime songs.

The summer was a bit more restful, except for one visit to Westminster School to talk about my wartime experiences. I kicked a football from my wheelchair for the first time in decades.

A Westminster schoolboy, aged eight, asked me if the Americans bombed everything like they do now. No, no, I told him. The Americans brought only manpower to the First World War. Their rifles had to be rebored to take British ammo. Eventually, the French supplied guns for them and the British had to reduce the number of horses to each British gun wagon in order to send animals over to the Americans, to pull their guns. It was all the Americans had at the time.

In October I was proud to open a building which was named after me. It was built on the site of a Fleet Air Arm station at Ford in West Sussex.

I knew Dennis had been trying to arrange a reunion of veterans from other European countries, but most of the men had physical difficulties that made foreign travel impossible. However, at the end of October, I was taken to the German town of Witten, near Dortmund, to meet my German counterpart.

Robert Meier was 109, a veteran of the fighting at the Somme. As I pointed out, I didn't see him there. He'd also met Kaiser Wilhelm II. Robert said it was amazing that we were both still alive. He asked, 'Why did we have to have a war? It is good to see people happy, to see us here together.'

I was very happy to meet my German counterpart. No man who knows war wants war again. I want to forget it. I knew that the Germans didn't want war any more than we did. The people themselves had no ill feelings towards us. Neither did we to them. I did not think too badly of the German people. They were like us, believing right was on their side and doing what they were told to do, just like us. When I finally arrived in Germany after the war, people were good to me.

Mind you, the war was over, Germany had been defeated and I was only involved with civilians who had not taken part in the fighting itself. In England there were many prisoners of war working on farms. They did a good job, as I was told.

Together, Robert and I placed a wreath in memory of our dead comrades at the local war memorial. There was a delegation there to represent the three French veterans who had been unable to travel.

Robert Meier was born in March 1897 in Ukraine, then part of the Russian Empire, to German parents. He enlisted as a soldier in 1916 and fought in France. In July 1918 he was shot in the leg and evacuated back to Germany, which is where he heard about the armistice four months later.

After the Second World War broke out, he was called up and ran logistics in a German camp. Just two weeks before the end of the conflict, with his family in eastern Germany, he was captured by the Russians and sent to a prisoner of war camp, where conditions were notoriously cruel. For three years he was out of contact with family and friends, trading cigarettes for food in order to survive. He was released in 1948. He had two children with his wife, Ella, who died in 1967.

Revealing a vibrant sense of humour, Robert was pictured on his 109th birthday, in March 2006, wearing a spiked German military hat and a T-shirt that read: '109 – na und?', meaning '109 – so what?' At the time, he was still living alone and caring for himself. However, after suffering a fall at Christmas 2006, his previously robust health declined sharply and he died in January 2007.

I spent Armistice Day in France in 2006, at St-Omer, laying a wreath at the memorial before attending Mass in the cathedral. The following week I saw the Battle of the Somme recreated at the Imperial War Museum. November finished with me meeting the pupils of Cavendish School, Eastbourne, to answer questions from pupils.

In December it was back to St James's Palace for the Not Forgotten Association's Christmas party. Later the same month, Dennis, Brenda and I went to the Fleet Air Arm station at Yeovilton to present Navy Wings to student pilots and observers graduating from the Lynx helicopter course. One of the pilots was a German Navy officer on an exchange visit. I was thankful to be part of a ceremony that binds all nations close together. I said well done and respected him for what he had achieved, alongside our countrymen.

The month was marred only by news of the death of Captain Kenneth Cummins, a very popular man. He was remembered in one of the speeches at the ceremony in Yeovilton where we also held a two minute silence in his memory.

Captain Kenneth Cummins, who died aged 106, served in two world wars and witnessed some of the momentous events of both. He was the last surviving Royal Navy officer from the First World War.

Cummins was born in 1900 and educated at Merchant Taylor's School in Crosby. He helped one of the pioneers of flight, Claude Grahame-White (1879–1959), to get airborne by holding and then releasing the rope that anchored his single-engine biplane. Grahame-White later achieved the first night flight carried out in Britain.

Keen to serve in the First World War, Cummins applied to join P&O as a naval cadet at the age of 15. His interview included a silver service dinner, in order to prove that his manners were sufficiently polished. Then, aged 18, he trained on HMS Worcester.

During the First World War, he saw a Zeppelin shot over the Thames, the bodies of American soldiers who had died from Spanish flu being carried off a ship and the bodies of Canadian nurses killed when their ship was illegally sunk by a U-boat. It was his first voyage on the armed cruiser HMS Morea.

His Majesty's Hospital Ship Llandovery Castle, *bearing its Red Cross insignia, was approaching Fastnet Rock, off the south coast of Ireland, in June 1918 when it came under attack. Not only was the ship sunk, but the survivors who took to lifeboats were shelled and rammed by the rogue U-boat. More than 230 people died, including 14 Canadian nurses. Much later, Cummins recalled:*

> We were in the Bristol Channel, quite well out to sea, and suddenly we began going through corpses. The Germans had sunk a British hospital ship, the *Llandovery Castle*, and we were sailing through floating bodies. We were not allowed to stop – we just had to go straight through. It was

quite horrific, and my reaction was to vomit over the edge.

It was something we could never have imagined . . . particularly the nurses: seeing these bodies of women and nurses, floating in the ocean, having been there some time. Huge aprons and skirts in billows, which looked almost like sails because they dried in the hot sun.

There was no chance of rescuing them – they were all dead. As the fighting ship – which we were – we were not permitted to stop unless ordered to do so by the Admiralty.

Between the wars, Cummins returned to work at P&O as a merchant officer. On one memorable occasion he was a watchkeeper in the steamship Macedonia, *which brought Lord Carnarvon's body to England in 1923. Carnarvon had financed the archaeological investigations that finally uncovered the tomb of Tutankhamen. His death was widely seen as confirmation of a curse issued centuries before by the Pharaoh – but is more likely to have been from the effects of a mosquito bite.*

At the start of the Second World War, P&O ships were commandeered as troop carriers and Cummins remained chief officer on the converted liner Viceroy of India. *After delivering troops for the North African invasion in 1942, during Operation Torch, the ship was shaken by a torpedo blast. It was Cummins' job to search the ship before it was abandoned. The noise of water rushing through the torpedo hole haunted him for the rest of his days.*

Cummins retired from P&O in 1960, having married five years previously. He died in December 2006.

One day, in the middle of a quiet patch, Dennis asked me how I liked my present way of life. I told him: 'I'm sitting pretty.'

It must be Dennis that decides what I do. Without him and Brenda, I could not go anywhere. I can't see enough, hear enough or get myself there.

I look forward to our visits. Mind you, sometimes I don't know where I'm going. But I've got used to that now and I like it. What else can I do? I'm in their hands. And some people never get out and I would hate that.

I hope I have never let the side down. I cannot remember like I used to and Dennis has to help me out. I tell him, you must get fed up with me. The thing is this, I like going to schools and also to the Navy and the RAF. It's a new lease of life. I tell Dennis: 'Put it in the diary. I'll be ready.'

Dennis assures me he has never taken me for granted and I believe him. Look at what he has done for all the veterans, not just me. He avoids last-minute appointments so I can take everything in my stride or, as he puts it, the circumference of my wheelchair.

A little research established that the Narrow Seas Club was still very much shipshape and Bristol fashion. When he was told about Henry, the skipper of the club extended an invitation to Henry to attend the club's 75th anniversary fitting-out dinner at the Royal Corinthian Yacht Club, Burnham-on-Crouch, Essex, on Saturday, 21 April 2007. Henry, Dennis and Brenda made the journey from Brighton by car. David Gray, Henry's eldest grandson, and his wife, Charlotte, were en route to Europe from America and they arranged a stopover in England. The two parties met up in Burnham-on-Crouch and, after catching up with the news from the US over lunch, they took Henry around Burnham. He recalled the name of a pub he had often frequented and related a few names associated with his sailing days in Burnham.

The Narrow Seas Club committee honoured Henry by inviting him to become honorary skipper, a post which had been vacant since the death of the club's final founder.

Every birthday for a super-centenarian is a special one. But after someone exceeds 110 years of age, the celebration of their birth assumes even greater significance. When he was 111, in a gesture of goodwill by the Royal Navy, Henry and guests celebrated aboard HMS Victory in Portsmouth. Once Nelson's flagship, it is now a popular historic feature in Portsmouth dockyard.

HMS Victory was launched in Chatham in 1765, some 227 ft long and fashioned from 2,000 oak trees. After being commissioned in 1778, the ship saw action in naval encounters across the globe but is best remembered for its role in the Battle of Trafalgar in 1805. The Victory retired from active service in 1812 and remained at anchor in Portsmouth Harbour for more than a century. The ship was still used by the Royal Navy in ceremonies. However, in 1922 it was moved into a dry dock following fears that the open sea was undermining its structure. After that, the Victory was renovated to eighteenth-century standards. It is now the flagship of Vice-Admiral Adrian Johns, Commander-in-Chief Naval Home Command, and is the last remaining ship of the line from that era.

The ship was a striking setting for a party, though a little challenging to manoeuvre Henry and his wheelchair around. Before retiring to dinner, Henry was treated to a display by the Royal Marines Band and a fly-past of aircraft old and new. He inspected the men and women of the band, congratulated them on their musical prowess and delivered four blows to the bass drum. Then he was piped aboard, and delivered to Nelson's Great Cabin by some sailors on hand for the task. Although it is usual for everyone on board to remain seated for the Queen's toast, due to a traditional shortage of headroom and rough seas, Henry insisted that everyone 'be upstanding'. Lieutenant Commander John Scivier said:

It was an absolute delight and pleasure to have Henry on board on this very special day for him and his family. It is very sobering to think that when Henry was born, *Victory* still had nearly 30 years of life left on open water. It is also remarkable to think that while we were all celebrating the Trafalgar bicentennial two years ago, Henry was already nine years old when they celebrated the centennial.

Later, there was a party hosted by Henry at a hotel, at which a helper, Graham Stark, sang a song he had composed, dedicated to the centenarian, and Nicola McAuliffe also serenaded him.

Henry is thought to be the world's second-oldest man after teetotaller Tomoji Tanabe from Japan, who is three months older. However, Henry shares his accolade with an American born on the same day – George Rene Francis, who now lives in California but was born and brought up in New Orleans.

Hardly a model of healthy living, George has always sworn by a diet of pork, eggs, milk and lard, and didn't give up smoking cigars until 1971, when he was 75 years old. George can recall being a passenger on buses when black people like himself were compelled to sit at the back, screened from fellow white travellers. It wasn't until he was in his 60s that the fight for racial equality in America began to make progress. He was a chauffeur for a white doctor, driving a Studebaker and a Cadillac. George was also once a keen fisherman. He is now the oldest living American. Despite his advancing years, he has retained an interest in baseball and basketball, which he follows on television.

We went to visit RAF Leeming in North Yorkshire in late June 2007. But it was chaos at Kings Cross, where we were catching the train. Eventually we got on board, but as we neared our destination, Dennis and Brenda realised the train was not stopping at North

Allerton as scheduled. They discovered from a guard that the station stop had been axed to help make up time on the delayed service. Dennis explained that a deputation of RAF personnel would be waiting at the station to meet us. Finally arrangements were made to go by car at York to RAF Leeming. But the poor welcoming committee from RAF Leeming had some heart-stopping moments when I failed to turn up on the train as promised.

After lunch in the airmen's mess, I met Tornado pilots. Sitting in an ejector seat, I told them it was a lot easier for them to fly planes than it was in my day. Today it is a case of turn the key and you're off. When I did it, we had to hold the tail, swing the prop and remove the chocks.

In July myself and veteran William 'Bill' Stone went to Buckingham Palace for a private audience with the Queen. We were introduced to Prince Charles and Camilla, the Duke of Kent, Princess Alexandra, Prince Edward and his wife, Sophie, and then the Queen and Prince Philip. Within a week, I was back at Buckingham Palace for the Not Forgotten Association's annual garden party.

For years I had suffered from a cyst on my backside. I often used to ask Dennis to get me a knife and a mirror so I could cut it out myself. That autumn I finally had surgery to have it removed and I made a quick recovery. Shortly afterwards, Dennis went into hospital to have surgery on a serious back condition, probably caused by years of wheeling around veterans like myself.

In August I met up with Harry Patch, the last army veteran from the First World War, and William Stone, a navy man. Although communication is difficult, it is always a great pleasure to be in their company – all organised by Dennis.

The following month I was at the *Pride of Britain Awards*, nominated by the public for special recognition. I had no idea why I was chosen but Dennis explained it like this:

It was a thank you by the general public, endorsing all the effort you have put in and all the time you have spent travelling the country as a crusader, reminding this nation of ours, especially its youth, of the sacrifices made by your generation not only during the most horrendous war experienced by mankind, but also the struggle and hardships facing these heroes during the depression of the 1920s, which was attributable to the war.

You have visited schools and breathed life into the pages of history. You have visited the stations and barracks of our serving armed forces, encouraging them by your bravery in the Great War and your fortitude today. You are an ambassador representing not only your generation, with your visits to France and Germany, but serving members of Her Majesty's Armed Forces. You are a brave man, Henry.

I felt like a real celebrity on the night, among an audience filled with stars.

In September 2007 I visited St-Omer in France where I laid five wreaths at five different memorials in the space of one day. I returned in November for the Armistice Day ceremony. While I was there, I went to visit Ypres and found myself in Poperinge. A crowd of people from Toc H, both British and Belgian, came to meet me.

Clearly, 2008 was going to be a big year. In March it was the 90th anniversary of my marriage to Dorothy. The following month saw the 90th birthday of the Royal Air Force, the world's first independent air force. In June I would celebrate my 112th birthday, while in November it would be time to mark the 90 years since the end of the Great War – the war to end all wars.

I told Dennis I didn't think I would be around for all the celebrations.

'Well,' he said. 'I have to make some plans if you are not here. We will have to do without you – but it won't be the same. Who will say the Lord's Prayer at the Cenotaph? I don't think there is anyone who will do it so well as you, so keep taking your water tablets. I know you keep telling me you are ready to go, but remember your manners. You have to be asked.'

My first public appearance of the year was at Gad's Hill School in Higham, Kent, in a house that used to be the home of writer Charles Dickens.

'I have always wanted to learn,' I told the children. 'If there was something I didn't understand I went out and found out how to understand it. You must learn and always do what your mother tells you.'

One of the highlights for Henry was to sign Certificates of Promotion for those boys and girls who were members of the Combined Cadet Force. It gave him a true sense of purpose to personally hand out the promotions to Lance Corporals and Corporals. Recipients were equally proud and delighted at Henry's sincerity and his high esteem of all those wearing the Queen's uniform.

Dennis put a health warning on all my engagements. 'Whenever you feel that you are not deriving any benefits from events that I have arranged for you,' he said, 'then you must call a halt. I will always try to guarantee a proactive role for you while I feel you are more than capable of fulfilling your engagement to the satisfaction of all those around you.'

It was obvious to Dennis that Henry's physical condition was declining and he needed much more support. There is inevitably some concern for Henry's well-being as time marches on, extending the limit of man's biblical three-score-years-and-ten to what must be now near breaking point. More importantly, though, Henry is still able to participate and enjoy this extended journey through life.

We returned to my flat in Eastbourne to pick up the post and check it over. Then I had fish and chips in the shopping centre, as I used to love to do. When I pushed my empty plate aside, I told Dennis and Brenda: 'That is the first full meal I have eaten this year. I have been off my food for some time.'

Still, I was fit enough to go to the Gielgud Theatre in London to see Nicola McAuliffe appear in *The Mikado*. It took me back to the happy days I spent in the theatres in London. I never for one moment believed I would enjoy a show like that again.

Then we went to the House of Lords. We met Baroness Boothroyd and Lord Craig, who told us the history of the House. As it was Shrove Tuesday, pancakes were on the menu for lunch. My appetite reappeared and the pancakes for dessert were just as good as the ones my nanna used to make for me.

An internet organisation called TrueTube, *which is a division of the Foundation for Christian Communication, a registered charity, wished to interview Henry for a short film looking at different generations of people who have served in the armed forces. Dennis went to Brighton to collect Henry and brought him to his home in Rustington, West Sussex. The camera crew had already arrived at the Goodwin studio and Henry was soon in full flow giving his opinions and experiences of the First World War. Dennis took his seat in front of the camera to answer similar questions about the Second World War. Brenda, in the meantime, prepared lunch as requested by Henry: macaroni cheese, his favourite dish, followed by fruit and ice cream.*

203

Soon afterwards, Henry was invited to Headley Court, the rehabilitation centre for servicemen and -women who have suffered injuries in Afghanistan, Iraq and other conflicts. Once again, Henry's aged, impaired body faced with equal dignity those whose bodies had been mutilated through the brutality of war.

During the conversations that ensued, Henry led the way with anecdotes about the First World War. What was soon apparent, according to onlookers, was the difference between Henry's visit and those of others. His restricted vision shielded him from the full extent of people's injuries and he listened to their voices rather than observed their disabilities and the limitations imposed on them by their wounds.

In March 2008 I met with Harry Patch and William (Bill) Stone at Bill's residential home in Wokingham, Berkshire. We talked about what would happen on 11 November 2008, the 90th anniversary of the end of the war. All of us wanted to take part in the proposed service of remembrance, if we were spared. The same month I was filmed by French television after the death of Lazare Ponticelli, aged 110, the last French veteran of the 1914–18 war.

When Dennis goes to see Henry, he invariably finds him slumped in his wheelchair, half asleep, with his head resting to one side. Dennis simply takes his hand, gives it a slight squeeze and watches as Henry immediately shows signs of recognition.

'How's the lad?' Henry asks. Then he says, 'Where's the girl?'

Right on cue, Brenda gives him a cuddle and they are all together again. One morning Dennis asked Henry, 'How are you feeling today?'

'I'm on top form,' Henry replied. 'I must be careful I don't fall off.'

Whenever Dennis and Brenda go anywhere unaccompanied by Henry, people who know them always ask: 'How's Henry?' There's no mention of Dennis or Brenda or how they are getting on. Dennis remarked, 'I wish I had an apple for every time people said that, so I could open a cider-making business.'

Before the anniversary of the RAF's formation, I went with Dennis and Brenda to the RAF Museum at Hendon to take part in a ceremony. As we parted, Dennis told me we were all going off to church on Sunday – to St Clement Danes in London, the central church of the Royal Air Force – for a service to mark the formation of the RAF.

Dennis was alarmed to receive a telephone call informing him that Henry had had an accident, having trapped his finger between his bed and the wall. He had been to hospital to have his finger examined and was now back at his home in Ovingdean, with the finger bandaged. Dennis and Brenda found Henry looking better than they had expected, but still decided to call off his engagements for the coming week.

'I'm all right,' Henry insisted. 'I only cut my finger. They said I have to keep it still.' As he said it, he waggled the injured finger under Dennis' nose. 'Go and have a word with them, tell them how important it is for me to go on Sunday.'

But it was not to be, and Dennis and Brenda had the eerie experience of attending an event without Henry.

On Monday, however, Henry received a green light to attend the main RAF commemorative event – their 90th anniversary celebration. Henry was the guest of honour. David, Henry's grandson, was in Britain on business and joined them all for the event. He always gets a particularly joyous welcome from Henry. On this occasion, he saw Henry the raconteur in action as he entertained the crew of a grounded Chinook helicopter from RAF Odiham. That evening they watched the Beating of the Retreat and a fly-past before David left for Gatwick to catch his flight to the USA.

The dessert that night was bread and butter pudding served with clotted-cream ice cream. Even after the last morsel had disappeared, Henry searched every bit of his bowl in a vain attempt to find just one more mouthful. Back at the hotel, he asked Dennis how he had performed. 'Just being there was a monumental performance. You did it with determination, grit and humour,' Dennis told him. Henry countered that he had done it all as a wounded hero as he looked at his bandaged hand.

Henry often reminisces about Rolls Royce cars. He takes pride in relating how his modifications helped Rolls Royce achieve Best Model at an international show in London. In early 2008, a neighbour asked a colleague who owned a Rolls Royce dating from the mid-1920s if he would take Henry for a spin. Just after lunch one day, the owner, Alan Appleford, arrived in the splendid vehicle. While Dennis pondered the best way to get the veteran into the vehicle, Henry was having different ideas.

'I'm not going in the car,' he announced. Alan and Dennis were dismayed until he continued, 'I want to have a good look at the car first. Take me round the other side.'

He quizzed Alan on every aspect of the car's history and maintenance before going for a trip into Worthing, causing quite a stir with passers-by. When he was back home, Henry confessed it was one of the most exciting moments he had experienced in decades. He hadn't thought for a second that he would be able to capture again those memories of working with Rolls Royce cars.

'I can't describe how I felt in that car,' he said. 'I was at my best when I worked with Rolls' and I was sorry when custom-built cars gave way to standard ones.'

That was when Henry decided to join Ford's in their experimental department. When he told Dorothy, she replied, 'That's nice, dear.' Henry said, 'I'm sure if I had told her I was going to start work at the local garage, I would have had the same reply.'

Soon afterwards, Dennis and Henry went to visit the Eton Mission Rowing Club. Henry had joined the club before the First World War, when his grandfather and Uncle Charlie were already members. He was often taken there in his youth and recalled riding his bike along the path by the River Lea, trying to overtake Uncle Charlie as he rowed.

I really enjoyed my days on the river. A long time ago I met a man who had just retired and lived near the River Thames. He had bought a boat and intended to see out his life sculling each day. I often think of that man and how much I envied him.

One of the best moments of my life was when the Honourable Johnson, the President of the Eton Mission Rowing Club, was officiating at a prize-giving ceremony and I was in the crew. The Honourable Johnson announced that there was a certain young man who had done remarkably well for himself. He had been successful in almost all the events he had entered. To my complete surprise, that young man was me. I took the vouchers I had won to Fishers the Jewellers, but instead of getting a trophy, I opted for things for the home.

Before their visit, Dennis got in touch with club secretary Jim Hinchcliffe, who looked back through the club's records. Henry's name was included in the minutes of 1914, which recorded the results of the Gig Handicap that year. Henry was second behind G. W. D'Arcy, with Uncle Charlie way down the order.

When they got to the rowing club, Henry noticed immediately that it was a new boathouse on the other side of the river to the original. A plaque revealed that the Johnstone Boat House had been presented to the Eton Mission Rowing Club by their President, Honourable Gilbert Johnstone, in memory of his Etonian Wet-Bob Brothers, Lord Derwent, the Hon. Cecil and Hon. Sir Alan Johnstone.

When it came to Henry's 112th birthday, in June 2008, it was the turn of the Royal Air Force to play host. RAF Cranwell was taken over for the day by Henry; eight of his grandchildren and great-grandchildren; friends; Brenda and Dennis; a phalanx of photographers, cameramen and reporters; some young officer cadets; and some of the British forces' top brass. Although a planned parachute jump had to be called off due to low cloud, the fly-past by the Battle of Britain Memorial Flight went ahead, to Henry's great delight. This event received worldwide coverage and was even shown on national television news networks – such is Henry's notoriety and the warmth and affection in which he is held.

On the evening of Henry's birthday, his first words to Dennis were: 'What's next?'

When he told him it was Trooping the Colour, Henry said, 'Good, I'll enjoy that. My mother took me when I was seven years old in 1903 and we had seats. How she got the tickets I'll never know. I often thought I would like to go again.'

After that, Henry went to Veterans' Day in Blackpool and to Fairford in Gloucestershire for another RAF celebration, avoiding unseasonal deluges when he could.

Curiously, the last two events before Henry's birthday – the trip in the Rolls Royce and the visit to the rowing club – seemed to touch him more deeply than any of the others. He seems more susceptible to nostalgia than in previous years.

At the time, many people were asking Dennis what to buy Henry for his birthday. His material needs are few now. Henry shrugged when they spoke about it, 'At one time, I could have given them a list as long as my arm, but now . . .

'But I can tell you this,' he continued. 'The trip to the rowing shed was the best birthday present I could ever have. You don't know what that meant to me and how much I enjoyed something I never thought could ever happen again, after all these years.'

Dennis squeezed his hand and Henry gave him a special smile, one he keeps for occasions like this. It was reward enough.

thirteen

HENRY AND DENNIS – A SPECIAL FRIENDSHIP

EVERYBODY SEEMS TO BE making a great fuss of me. I must say I like it. But I can't believe it is true – not in my wildest dreams did I think I would reach this great age. I had 53 years of happy marriage and two daughters. These were the best things that happened in my life. I've always taken pleasure in familiar company, the right sort of company. I wouldn't want my life to have been any different.

I feel I lived through two specific eras for the first 14 years of my life, the Victorian and Edwardian. But no one else has coined a phrase for the rest of it. In some ways, it was the best part.

When I found out Harry Patch had written his life story, I asked Dennis to help me do the same – as I feel I have a lot to pass on to the people who are interested in those times, and I think I might have something interesting to say myself. People generally want to know what happened in the period of the war years. I accept that and am willing to relate my involvement in the war as a means of keeping alive the memory of all those men and women of my generation who gave their all. I am the last one to answer the call so to speak.

Dennis says, Henry is special. Not only is Henry enormously resilient, but he has something different to offer.

'I don't know what it is but he is a unique man. He is at complete ease when he is speaking to other people and he is sincere in what he says. You have to see the relationship he has had with people at large, whoever they are – anyone from the Queen to high-ranking forces officers and Members of Parliament. I tell him he should have been a diplomat. I say he should have been a hit with the girls. "I am now," he tells me. "And it's too late." But he isn't smooth. And he has the same effect on everybody. It is that chemistry that just endears him to everybody, even those who are sometimes a bit starchy. It is something aside from his great age.'

Henry has been collecting his pension for 47 years now. That alone is a splendid achievement, without taking any of the other things he does into consideration. It includes travelling long distances, talking to children and describing events that happened scores of years ago.

Although people want to know about my service record, Dennis pointed out that I was also an observer. In the early days of the war, I was a civilian waiting to join up, relying on information from newspapers, local gossip and hearsay. Later, in France, my involvement behind the lines meant I could talk to infantrymen, gunners and field ambulance personnel. I visited French camps and American units. I really had no business to be there, but it was my quest for knowledge of what was happening around me that made me go the extra mile.

Dennis is the only man I have ever met, other than veterans themselves, who has a genuine empathy for those who served. Over the past seven years or so I have spent a great deal of my time with him and his family. He takes me to all my many events and has been my ears and eyes. It is he who can now get my message across to younger generations.

I have always said it was the men in the trenches that suffered, it was the men in the trenches who in my view won the war. So I feel I don't deserve all this attention. Other men did so much more than me. We owe them so much – they sacrificed their future so that we all might have one, I firmly believe that. We have got to thank the men who gave all they could on my behalf and on your behalf and it's got to carry on happening. I wonder how the public would respond today if 19,000 people were killed in a single day, as they were at the Somme.

Whenever I visit anywhere new, I always seek out the war memorial and pay my respects. It was a kind of promise I made to myself that, if I was spared, I would try to remember those less fortunate. I simply stand to attention, take off my hat and bow my head, and my memories of the war come flooding back.

In four months' time who knows what condition I will be in but I want people to remember the sacrifices that were made. Sometimes I look back and I don't know how I had the neck or the cheek to do the things I did. They always came off. I was crazy. I have done it my way.

I have had a very good life, very happy, and I'm thankful for it. I appreciate it. There have been times when I have been dead scared, times when I should have been more scared than I was, only I didn't know it at the time. Only with hindsight do I look back and realise just how lucky I have been.

I'm not the kid I used to be, but I still get around. You make your own happiness, whatever age you are. Seeing the funny side of life is useful, and I've always had a sense of humour. People ask me, what's the secret of a long life? I don't know. People ask me how I've done it and I just say that I look forward to another tomorrow.

The trick is to look after yourself and always know your limitations. Each day is a good day in my book. But I owe it to those men who have died, to remind future generations of the supreme sacrifice they made.

Dennis firmly believes that Henry is unique, if only for his resurgence at the age of 105 years.

'It is true that I only got to know Henry really well over a comparative short period of time – some eight years ago. It did, give me some insight as to what kind of man he was – as I doubt I will ever know the true Henry of old. The man I met at the beginning of the Millennium at first sight showed very few signs of the ageing process. My association with the many veterans I have known has enabled me to make this comparison.

'On closer contact, his eyesight had now failed him allowing only peripheral vision and his hearing, even with an aid, was difficult though not impossible. His grip was strong and there was a sparkle in his eyes. He was, however, his own man and made it quite clear at the outset that he wanted nothing more than his own solitude.

'I had bought a copy of my current newsletter and asked Henry if I might continue to send him future issues just so we might stay in contact. I had learnt he was living alone as he had outlived his friends and associates, and the family he had left in touch resided in America. It was his perceived inability to lead the life he had enjoyed that somehow had convinced him that his life today had nothing left to offer him. Once Henry had accepted me for what I was, a relationship quickly developed. As with other veterans, I knew that to gain his respect and confidence, I had to be a good listener. Fortunately I had years of practice, and was adept at steering any conversation about painful wartime memories towards happier ones of family, career, hopes and ambition. Step by step, I gradually got to know Henry very well. The more private side of him unfolded during periods when I helped him prepare for sleep or whilst assisting him with his private necessities of daily life.

212

'Henry is essentially a self-made man. He realised fairly early on that the only way he was going to succeed in life was through his own endeavours. He was a loner with many refrains of 'I did it my way.' Henry has changed over the intervening years physically, but also with his general demeanour. His experiences over the last one hundred years or so has enabled him to adapt to new situations and people. His almost complete dependency on other people has diluted his 'my way' approach – with the exception that he knows his body better than anyone else.

'My interest in veterans who fought in the Great War goes back a long way. As part of my own career development, I transferred into the National Health Service in 1960. I was seconded to a large psychiatric hospital in Lancashire. I learnt that the majority of male patients in the wards I worked on, who were aged sixty years or more, were in fact Great War veterans. It was the trauma of their experience, which was the reason they were confined to closed-off wards with death often their only release. It saddened me and I felt some shame in being unable to do anything but witness their plight.

'It was however, much later on in my life that I was able to befriend veterans who by this time were entering the twilight of their years and for whom loneliness, and in some cases despair, were their specific everyday problems. At the beginning of the 1990s it became an almost full-time occupation. Arising from that first pilgrimage to Flanders in 1998 the veterans seemed to be turning up from all four corners of the country. Fortunately for me this began to happen before I had the chance to savour retirement but I was content to put it on hold for some time later on in my life.

'I was able to build up a network of helpers over the years – these were in the main the families of the veterans themselves who had sadly passed away as time went on. These helpers wished to continue their support to our growing organisation and proved to be an invaluable asset, contributing an enormous amount of energy, enthusiasm and success to the association.

'My time was spent organising reunions in many parts of the country and pilgrimages to Flanders. I wrote newsletters and corresponded with veterans and their families. I also managed to organise fundraisers to financially support the association as the years went by and our activities grew. I can recall many Henry Allingham types whom I was to befriend over this period – indeed over the past twenty years it has been my honour and a privilege to gain the friendship and trust of so many remarkable men and women. Their names may not mean much to you the reader, but they have meant so much to me in my life that is much the richer for having known them and shared their memories.

'Looking back and to my immediate relationship with Henry I would like to think that in some small way I have managed to bring into his life, and other veterans before him, opportunities that have reawakened their belief that life had much more to offer and that these opportunities had to be special to bring them out of themselves. From laying a wreath at the Tomb of the Unknown Soldier in Paris; to a commemorative service in Westminster Abbey; numerous events at Sandringham, and Buckingham Palace; and many other distinguished places and events.

'Veterans whose longevity was commented upon over the past two decades, have one thing in common with Henry. Following each event or occasion they asked the same question, "When is the next event, I'll be ready." Henry himself just tells me "Put it in the diary," and I have many letters from their loved ones confirming that this continued focus of attention to the next event prolongs and benefits these veterans final years.

'The spectre of psychiatric wards is still with us today. It has enabled me to focus on the individuals themselves and not just their military service in the Great War, however dramatic and traumatic that was for many of them. This period of their lives, when compared with their actual longevity, is just a fraction, but it has left a life-long mark on them. There has always been a reluctance with so many, but not all, to talk about the war. Strangely enough, put half a dozen of them in a room together, a few pints of beer (not compulsory) and the lamp will swing. This focus on the individual sets us apart from other organisations, together with our pledge that we will endeavour to make every effort for these veterans to make the pilgrimage to Flanders in spite of any physical infirmities or logistical problems. If they have the will and the courage to attempt the journey, we will ensure they get there – this holds true today as demonstrated by Henry.

'Quite recently, the following question was put to me regarding Henry's trips. "How would you feel if Henry died whilst he was being driven in a car or on a train or at a function? Surely it would be better for him to die peacefully at home?" I replied that I would be happy for him secure in the knowledge that he was, at the time of death, living his life as he wanted to.

'I can remember the first veteran of my acquaintance who reached a century. I was due to take him to an armistice parade, the weather was cold, wet and windy. I must admit to some apprehension as to his well being and so telephoned his daughter and voiced my concerns. Her reply was "I have got him all wrapped up, long johns and all. He should be fine but if something did happen to him, that's the way he would like to go – with the banners and flags waving and drums and bugles playing, his comrades at his side."

'At the beginning of our relationship Henry was still reluctant to talk about his wartime experiences. I knew that his war service would sooner or later attract the attention of the media, who at that time knew very little of him, or indeed any of the veterans. Anticipating that this might cause him problems and possibly distress, I decided to take him to meet other Great War survivors. They readily conversed with him about their experiences and encouraged Henry to talk about his own war. After several visits Henry confessed that he had really enjoyed meeting them observing that "he had a lot to be thankful for," and equally commenting upon the relationship he could see I had with them, and they enjoyed with me.

'After one visit to the veterans, Henry later asked, " 'Smiler' Marshall tells me you took him to a school to talk to the children?" I replied I had, adding 'I think it is important to veterans that they should be recognised.' I believe by encouraging these visits, over time it does help increase their self-esteem – and this has been one of my chief principals in working with the veterans over time. Equally, it is also a great benefit to the teachers and pupils alike to have a living piece of history walk into their classrooms and bring their Great War studies to life – thus reinforcing the written word with actual anecdotes from the real thing.

'The schools are asked to prepare their own questions to ask Henry involving the whole of his life, and his opinion on anything in general really. There is usually one session in the morning of about 45 minutes – followed by lunch – and then a further session in the afternoon. The questions are asked by the pupils themselves and they often refer to a specific event in Henry's life which I can quietly ask him to relate back to them. Other questions I repeat verbatim into Henry's 'good ear' and we go on from there. We are quite a double-act and I can see the children enjoy these sessions – the children reading just as much from Henry's face as from his words. Often I try to steer Henry into relating the incident I had in mind once a question has been asked and slowly a broad smile crosses his face once he understands and off we go – his infectiousness for fun radiating out to the young audience, who are always very receptive to him.

'Henry was living in a flat, some forty miles from where I was living and he was therefore within easy reach for me to see him. I sifted through many requests from the media and other interested organisations, and from this a series of events were organised with him in mind. Some were conducted in Henry's flat in Eastbourne, but some involved travelling and on these occasions I would organise the transport – and there he would be, waiting to be picked up every time! I never questioned how long he had been ready nor did he volunteer any information, I would usually find him waiting, singing to himself to pass the time. Some trips there might be an overnight stay, and he would then be waiting for me with a suitcase packed.

'By Armistice Day of 2002 there were 44 Great War veterans remaining in Britain – and so with this news the media at last woke up to this significance and thus began what has been a rollercoaster of activity for the association and myself. I contributed to articles in the press featuring all the survivors who were now centenarians – this startling number now alerted me to the fact too that the days of befriending new veterans were themselves numbered. The veterans themselves were setting new landmarks in longevity. A reunion at the Public Records Office in Kew, London mustered nine men, their combined ages totalled 844 years!

Providence decreed that this unique generation had kept someone back to carry the torch – Henry Allingham. He became president of the Veterans Association and would prove to be a superb ambassador, travelling with me on countless journeys, both within the UK and abroad. Obviously, Brenda and I are there to support him at all times, and we keep his enthusiasm for the task at hand raised to a level he is comfortable with. The more birthdays he has – such as for his 112th this year – the greater the media spotlight intensifies. Henry was forever being asked the secret of his longevity, to which he famously replied, "cigarettes and whisky," a theory that provoked much amusement. I continually tell him to 'enjoy your birthdays, as the more you have the longer you'll live.' I know that right now he is not too far behind the record for the longest-lived man in British history [this record belongs to John Evans – born 19 August 1877 who died on 10 June 1990, aged 112 years and 295 days] as Henry is now 112 years and 86 days at the time of writing.

Alas, time catches up with everyone. Over the past two years, Henry has shown signs of slowing down and it is a great effort on our part to get him from A to B. Each appointment has to be carefully organised and selected according to how he may be feeling, or what kind of transport we can organise. Car journeys can be fraught as they cause Henry some distress, and we have found the train to be the best method of getting him to his appearance without causing any undue headaches for all concerned. The journeys to France have never been a problem with the RAF laying on transportation – their goal being to give Henry the most comfortable and relaxing trip possible. They have never let us down.

The main skill of being with Henry is to treat him as just another person, without airs or graces. His sight and hearing have been a problem over the years but he never shows it in public. Very early on he was concerned about not recognising people and it is here I aid him by identifying the person he will converse with, as well as try to give him a proactive role in these events, just to maintain his attention and desire to attend them. How long can he carry on doing these appearances? I really don't know, just as long as he is able to participate and understand where he is and what is being said to him, then I will continue to escort him and be his eyes and ears. I actually never solely rely on my own judgement in such matters, as Henry is quite capable of saying "enough is enough," and that is when we shall all call it a day. I do have these conversations with him to try and detect his feelings, as it is quite a responsibility. I am sure if there was a physical problem that curtailed his involvement I would see it coming myself, or be advised by his carers at the home for the blind at St Dunstans.

'As Henry himself commented before, "One day I am sitting alone with just four walls as my companions, then next I was wheeled into another world. My day is transformed beyond imagination and I am taken to places and to meet with people I normally would never encounter. The trust I have built over the years with Dennis enables me to build up a picture of where I am and what I am involved with to a degree, and for that I am grateful."'

'Henry would like to leave a legacy by which he could be remembered and it concerns the names of all those who survived the Great War. During the many pilgrimages and reunions made by these veterans to Flanders *and in Britain, services of remembrance were held at the local cenotaph – with the veterans themselves conducting the services. At the end of each service, as chairman of the association, I would recall the names of those veterans who had "gone over the top" since our last get-together. I would often think that in front of me on the monument were the names of those who had fallen, but what about those who had survived and were now dying? What monument was there to the survivors so future generations would know about their history? This is a topic I have often mulled over with Henry and how it seems people who meet him are connecting to their own families' history of the Great War – as the vast majority of us have a story to tell of a relative at that time.*

'It is the fashion nowadays for people to want to discover their family history – 'Who Do You Think You Are' on BBC1 sparked off a tremendous interest in this genre, and the internet has opened up immense possibilities. It is far easier today to discover one's ancestors and what they did in the Great War than ever before, after all, this all happened only 90 years ago. We should be using Henry's legacy as a starting point to educating the younger generations about this time and how it should never be allowed to happen again. Equally, it would be fantastic if we could encourage each local community across the country to keep a record of all those in their areas who fought and died in the war, and indeed the Second World War too. This could then be expanded into some charitable scheme to educate the next set of school children who want to know more about this period. We have a duty to keep this message alive once the likes of Henry are gone, which will be soon. It would be a tragedy if the nation moves on and forgets about the sacrifices his generation made and the message of peace and understanding they now promote.

'Perhaps the reason for my attachment to Henry is something to do with my own childhood and the questions I never asked my own father. I was brought up in a fire station and all the men there had fought in the First World War. As kids we played in the fire station,

although we never talked about the war because our parents never did. Often, when we had comics that focused on war or fighting, one of the men would say: "It wasn't like that." I had uncles who fought in the war and some who had died. Indeed, everyone knew somebody who had perished. But there were very few books on the conflict. Perhaps there had been immediately after the war, but there was nothing much in the 1920s and 1930s. It wasn't on the syllabus in schools either. I knew far more about the Napoleonic Wars than ever I did about the First World War.'

fourteen

TESTIMONIES FOR HENRY

THE SPECIAL SIGNIFICANCE OF the veterans now is that they are a scarce commodity. Dennis remembers writing a newsletter in the mid-1990s saying: 'Your lives have been significant but the longer you live, the more significant they become.'

Air Vice-Marshal Peter Dye, director of the Royal Air Force Museum at Hendon, summed up Henry's appeal and the way he can readily move people between laughter and tears:

> I suspect many people see their own grandparents and great-grandparents in Henry and feel that, through him, they have an opportunity to express their personal feelings. The respect and emotion that surround Henry are therefore not just about what the nation owes to Henry and his generation (important though this is); most people who have met Henry regard him as part of their family.
>
> Standing to one side of Henry on numerous occasions, it never fails to amaze me how swiftly he touches a nerve in even the most steely bystanders.

Peter Dye first met Henry in September 2004 at the unveiling of the British Air Services Memorial at St-Omer. He had embarked on this project some three years before, with the aim of providing a permanent memorial to those airmen and airwomen from the British Air Services who had served on the Western Front during the First World War.

> Very late in the day, I was able to contact Dennis Goodwin and ask if Henry would like to join us at the dedication service. I was half-expecting to be told that this would be much too difficult a journey for a 108-year-old veteran, and so was delighted when Henry promptly agreed.
>
> The most poignant moment of the unveiling ceremony was when Henry, unaided, personally laid a wreath at the foot of the new memorial. This generated a spontaneous round of applause and quite a few tears. Henry's involvement made the day all the more significant and somehow bridged the gap between the cold stone and sharp bronze letters of the memorial and the flesh and blood of the young men it commemorated.

Afterwards, at a separate ceremony, Henry was made a freeman of the town of St-Omer in recognition of his personal contribution and on behalf of all those who had fought to defend France during the First World War. This began a close association that has continued with Henry regularly returning to St-Omer on Armistice Day as well as on the town's annual Liberation Day. It would be fair to say that Henry is greatly loved by everyone at St-Omer. They are extremely proud of their oldest citizen.

When it comes to character references for Henry, well, they all come from people who have known him most recently. There are no school chums alive today to recollect anecdotes from the playground. All of those men who served in the forces directly alongside Henry are gone. Work colleagues, close family, fellow golfers and fishermen have died, in some cases a lifetime ago.

Yet there has been no shortage of testimonials for Henry, probably because he has put more energy and effort into the years that came after his 100th birthday than many people give in the whole of their retirement. Even his grandson David admits to knowing him better as a super-centenarian than ever he did before. And it is to David that we turn for a very personal tribute. David, who is one of five children, was an accountant who joined a bakery business and finally rose to be President of the Sara Lee sweet goods company. After he retired aged 40, he sat on a number of company boards of directors. But his first memory of Henry comes as a very small child.

> My mother, Jean, was a war bride, and although my older sister was born in England, she came to the States aged four months. My first recollection of Henry is when he came over in the early 1950s when I was still in a stroller and took me to the local zoo. He and my grandmother travelled on the *Queen Mary*, the same ship that took my mother to the States as a GI bride.
>
> Given the distance and the fact that our family didn't have the money to travel back and forth, I don't think I saw him again until 1969.

Nonetheless, David's mother, who had dual British-American citizenship, ensured that David and his siblings were aware of their roots.

> I remember sitting down in front of a flickering television set when I was five years old, when my mother made us watch the Queen's coronation.
>
> My memory of Dorothy is short. She always had a smile on her face but she was very quiet. He was the stronger personality.

The last time we saw her in 1969 she was ill, although we didn't know it at the time. But apparently that was the reason for their visit. This time they travelled on the *Queen Elizabeth*.

Through stories told by his mother, David has built up a picture of the life Henry and his family led in England during the 1930s and 1940s.

My mother and her sister went to a private Catholic girls' school even though my grandparents were not Catholic. My mother remembered getting a spanking before heading off for school, in preparation, so I think Henry and my grandmother were relatively strict.

My grandmother ran a little grocery store at the time. The girls worked there. After they finished school, it was wartime and my mother and her sister worked in London. My mother worked at the Colonial Office while my Aunt Betty worked in Churchill's Foreign Office.

It was Jean who spent much of her spare time in the company of her sports-loving father. David recalls:

She was pretty much his best friend. He used to love to sail. The two of them spent weekends on the water during the spring and summer months. My grandmother and my aunt weren't that interested in sailing so he relied on my mother as his crew. I think she was his favourite.

In fact, my mother's first love was horseback riding. When she came over from England, she brought with her riding boots, jodhpurs and a riding crop. But she never got to use them as my father was on a relatively low income as a civil servant and it was a challenge on a moderate budget.

When the bombs first started falling during the Second World War, the family would all go into a shelter. Finally the bombing became so frequent, they gave up and stayed in bed. They believed if they were going to get hit, they were going to get hit. Eventually they moved to Epping Forest, to an aunt's house in Woodford Wells.

My father was a tail gunner in the 8th US Army Air Force, flying B17s. He was as much a son to my grandfather as my mother was his daughter. Henry really enjoyed it when my father brought fellow airmen to visit from time to time. He talks as much about my father now, and about the conditions those boys flew in, with no radar, terrible weather and high mortality rates.

David's father, Lonny, died in 1993, aged 70, while Jean died in 2001, aged 78.

As Henry approached retirement, he and Dorothy purchased a flat in Eastbourne in a new construction that Henry still owns today. He lived there for the better part of 50 years. Yet, as David has discovered in numerous meetings, Henry's mind is still focused on the First rather than the Second World War or beyond.

Most of his stories are about the First World War, when he would ride in biplanes with bombs on his lap and drop them overboard near the targets. It was very primitive. We had the opportunity to see some of the planes he flew in and worked on when we went to his 112th birthday celebrations. I was pretty amazed that they even flew.

When it comes to his incredible lifespan, David believes Henry's approach to living has been entirely intuitive.

He has always been healthy. He has walked a tremendous amount and played golf, walking the course, pulling his clubs. Even when he was aged over 90, he would only buy half of his groceries at a time, so that he had to make two trips, just to get the exercise. He has always eaten a lot of home-grown vegetables, nothing processed at all. He wasn't a heavy drinker and, although I believe he was once a smoker, he did not smoke in his later years. Once he had a small amount of skin cancer on his nose, which was removed and never came back. Other than that he has barely been ill during 11 decades.

But it is Henry's personality, rather than his extraordinary longevity, that evokes the greatest emotions in people. David explains:

> I have got to know him since he turned 100 and I have found him to be one of the nicest people I know. He is very positive, very sparkling and always with a twinkle in his eye. It is not unusual for him to break out into song because he feels like it or to start telling a joke.
>
> When we meet him, he discusses not only family but other people we have introduced him to. He always wants to know what they are doing, always trying to take the attention away from himself and give it to others.

Henry is passionately interested in his American family. He has five grandchildren, twelve great-grandchildren, nineteen great-great-grandchildren and one great-great-great-grandchild. Says David:

> He isn't dynamic, just a very steady, fun-loving family person who has led a life that we should all want to live. He had a lot of friends and he loved his family. He always had an interest in the political scene, although not so much lately. And he has always had tremendous respect for the Royal Family. A packed diary that would leave a man half his age breathless has much to do with his vigour.
>
> Dennis gets a lot of credit for his being alive today. Henry has a calendar by his chair at home. He will look at it two or

three times when I visit him, to see when his next appointment is. A year ago, at his 111th birthday, he told us he was going to die in July. When I saw him after that I asked him what had happened. He said, 'I had to go to the Queen's garden party.'

David believes there is a reason that Henry was kept alive – it is to sustain the memory of those who died. He recalls one recent incident:

During the luncheon to celebrate his 112th birthday, Henry decided he had to go to the toilet. I didn't see him for about 20 minutes so I set off to make sure he was all right. He had come across a group of schoolchildren who had come to sing to him. They collected around him and started to sing together. I heard at least five songs from them. Henry was singing right along with them. He probably had more interest in the kids than many of the people at the lunch.

Henry is an inspiration to others, and not just the young, according to Peter Dye.

For those like me, about to retire, Henry is a reminder that life does not stop at some arbitrary date and that you can continue to make a contribution at whatever age. Henry epitomises determination and perseverance and as such is a role model for all generations.

His effort to bear witness to what happened in the First World War is a noble and selfless endeavour. Watching Henry interact with schoolchildren (both in England and France), one is struck by the obvious empathy and the way that the children respond to his presence. It is as if the 100 or so years separating them simply melt way. I know that for my daughters, as for all children who have met him, he is simply a wonderful person – who is also prepared to break into song at any excuse, particularly when at the dinner table in a very posh restaurant. Individuals half his age would be congratulated for achieving half as much. Henry is a modest man, but an exceptional human being.

I continue to find it amusing that Henry's first attempt to get a valid passport to return to France in 2004 [for reasons of tourism] was rejected by the Passport Office because it was clearly a fraudulent application, whereas in 1915, he had had no such difficulty when he was clearly intent on employing violence to defeat the King's enemies.

The point is that Henry's vigour and energy serve to demolish stereotypes about old age. Just as I was surprised that a 108-year-old veteran could travel to France (rather than being confined to bed or restricted to a care home), so others have had to revise their views about what the elderly can achieve. In the present climate, this is a timely reminder that everyone, regardless of their age, demands our respect for what they have achieved and what they can continue to contribute to society. Of course, in Henry's case, he has been doing this for longer than virtually every other human on the planet.

Vice-Admiral Sir Adrian Johns is another friend of Henry's who can bear testament to his enduring appeal. He spoke after seeing him twice in a week this summer.

Last Tuesday he attended one of our annual garden parties at Admiralty House in Portsmouth and, as last year, he helped take the salute when the Royal Marines Band beat retreat and performed Ceremonial Sunset. And on Monday of this week, we met up in the House of Commons for afternoon tea as guests of Derek Twigg, Minister for Veterans.

Henry certainly gets about and it's fun to hang onto his coat tails. Henry has given me some good advice as well; I am soon to retire from the Royal Navy and when I mentioned this to

Henry, he simply said: 'Don't look back – just look forward.'
Excellent advice indeed.

There's no doubt in the Second Sea Lord's mind about the
contribution Henry has made throughout his life.

Henry fought for his country in the most difficult of
circumstances. He showed courage, commitment, selflessness,
resilience and a sense of humour in the face of adversity. These
same qualities we seek in our young people in the Navy today
and Henry is a living embodiment of these timeless values. He
gives young servicemen and -women a sense that they belong
to something that is far more than just a job. We can try and
teach history and heritage in the classroom but with Henry
you can touch it and hear it at first hand. Henry lives for each
day, hence his advice to me about always looking forward.

Henry is an inspiration because he is a living link with
history. For us in the Royal Navy, he is an icon because he
joined the Royal Naval Air Service as an Air Mechanic in 1915
and he is the only surviving member of the old RNAS and
indeed of the Great War Navy.

I took Henry to a Wings Parade at the Royal Naval Air
Station at Yeovilton a couple of years ago. He presented the
Wings [the flying badge] to those successful young people
who had just completed their flying training in the Royal
Navy. As each of them came forward, Henry pressed the
wings onto the sleeve of their uniform jacket and whispered
a few words into their ear. The hairs on the back of my
neck stood on end! It was a moving moment because it was
quite clear that Henry was passing on something much more
profound than just a cloth flying badge; something else was
being passed across the generations, something that those
young people on parade will carry with them for the rest of
their lives and those of us who witnessed it will remember

for a long time. This I believe demonstrated exactly the importance of our heritage. I recall a wise old Admiral saying to me once that I should never fear danger or the enemy, only letting down those who had gone before. This is the effect that Henry had that day.

Next year marks the centenary of Royal Navy aviation and we hope and pray that Henry will be with us to help celebrate our 100 years of flying over the sea. From me, the oldest naval aviator in the Royal Navy today, to Henry, the oldest naval aviator in the world, I wish him all the best and look forward to the next time we meet.

Author Max Arthur, who has interviewed Henry for some of his best-selling books about the First World War, said:

He is the last vestige of a life that no one else will live again. He is the sole survivor of the RNAS. He has conducted his life certainly in the last decade with enormous decorum, dignity and honour, and has give us an insight into a world no one else will see again.

He is wonderful with children. They hold his hand even though there is a 100-year difference in age. He can still get right into their world, as if he has never left it. He has an extraordinary, childlike approach to life, having dealt with a lot of cynicism and bitterness – and seen them off.

Air Vice-Marshal Peter Dye has particular insight into Henry's contribution to the modern Royal Air Force:

Henry is the last founder member of the Royal Air Force. As such, he is a direct link to those young men and women who helped create the world's first independent air service and who just 22 years later enabled us to win the Battle of Britain.

Henry's willingness to visit RAF stations, attend graduation parades and talk with those serving today allows us to better understand the values that have underpinned the Service from its inception. Henry has undoubtedly influenced many thousands of young trainees and continues to be an inspiration as well as a source of great pride. The values of Henry's generation – respect, integrity, service and excellence – remain as important today in the Royal Air Force as they were 90 years ago. Perhaps the most telling example of this has been his several unpublicised visits to Headley Court, where he has met injured veterans from both Iraq and Afghanistan.

To sum up Henry's charisma and personal magnetism is a tall order. Nonetheless, Peter Dye knows better than most just how capable Henry is when it comes to holding an audience in the palm of his hand.

Part of Henry's magic is that you can have a conversation with him. It is not just his age, but the way that you can talk about current affairs as well as the past. Clearly, the media never tire of asking him about the First World War – questions that he invariably addresses without rancour or lack of patience – but children find it fascinating that someone born in the reign of Queen Victoria can advise them about homework, as well as telling them what life was like in the trenches.

This is as true in Britain as it is overseas, and not just in France. When Henry visited Dortmund to meet with one of the last surviving German veterans, the reaction from all those he met was very similar. What was also remarkable was that the meeting of the two veterans was like a reunion of two old friends – with the same sense of humour!

EPILOGUE

IN HIS FINAL YEARS, Henry has confided in Dennis about what he thinks the future holds. Dennis recalls taking Henry down onto the beach in summer 2007 and asking him, 'Where do you think you are going to end up?'

Henry said he had no idea. He did believe there was some divine being but he didn't know what it was.

'If I tried to question it, I'm sure I could convince myself otherwise, so I don't,' Henry said. 'Look at the beach, that's where we will all end up. We will become part of the earth like a grain of sand and that is, in a way, being born again.'

When he was younger, Henry decided to donate his body to science. But that decision has changed as he has come to appreciate the increasing significance of his life and impending death. He knows the Ministry of Defence has been concerned about what to do when the last survivor from the First World War dies. The idea of a state funeral has been largely dismissed, but his passing is an event that will inspire the collective grief of the nation in a way that has been missing for several generations. With Henry, because of his standing in the media and with all his family in America, he realises that a ceremony is likely to fulfil a public need. In marking his passing, people will once again consider the sacrifices made by the rest of his generation during the First World War. His funeral is in the process of being organised.

Last year Dennis counted that Henry had clocked up 47 events, which is quite something for a man of his age. He is essentially a very private man. But a very wonderful one. Perhaps the last words belong to a First World War poet whose lines have often been quoted but never as poignantly as now:

> To you from failing hands we throw
> The torch; be yours to hold it high.
> If ye break faith with us who die
> We shall not sleep, though poppies grow
> In Flanders fields.

John McCrae (1872–1918)

TIMELINE OF WORLD EVENTS IN HENRY ALLINGHAM'S LIFE

LISTED HERE ARE THE major historical events that the majority of us have either been taught in school or have discovered as we grew older by reading newspapers, listening to radio broadcasts or watching television. The breadth of these events clearly reflects the incredible stretch of time that Henry Allingham has lived through – from a time of horse-drawn transport, gaslight and a greater sense of community, to one today of international travel, space-age communication and a greater sense of the individual, who can travel wherever he or she desires, send messages across the globe in seconds – and of course wage war in apocalyptic terms.

1896
Henry Allingham is born.

1900
The 3rd Marquess of Salisbury (Conservative) is re-elected Prime Minister.

1901
Queen Victoria dies and Edward VII succeeds to the throne.

1902
Second Boer War ends. Arthur Balfour (Conservative) replaces the 3rd Marquess of Salisbury as Prime Minister.

1903
Wilbur and Orville Wright fly a heavier-than-air machine for almost one minute, over a distance of 850 ft, in Kitty Hawk, North Carolina.

1905
Henry Campbell-Bannerman (Liberal) becomes Prime Minister.

1906
An earthquake in San Francisco kills at least 1,000 people.

1907
Boy Scout Movement is established by Robert Baden-Powell.

1908
Herbert Henry Asquith (Liberal) becomes Prime Minister.

1910
Edward VII dies and George V succeeds to the throne.

1912
The *Titanic* sinks in the Atlantic.

1913
The bodies of Captain Robert Falcon Scott and two others are discovered in Antarctica. Scott had recently come second in a race to the South Pole. Suffragette Emily Davison dies under the hooves of the King's horse at the 1913 Derby.

1914
First World War breaks out.

1915
The *Lusitania* is sunk by a German U-boat with the loss of 1,400 civilians.

1916
David Lloyd George (Liberal) becomes Prime Minister. The Easter Uprising takes place in Dublin. Tanks are used for first time by Allies on the Western Front. Conscription is introduced in Britain.

1917
The Russian Revolution results in Russia's withdrawal from the First World War. Wild-West hero 'Buffalo Bill' dies aged 72. The USA enters the First World War on the side of the Allies.

1918
Tsar Nicholas II and his family are executed in Russia. The First World War ends.

1919
An epidemic of Spanish flu that has caused the deaths of as many as 100 million people worldwide comes to an end.

1921
Unemployment benefit in Britain increases as the jobless total stands at more than a million. Charlie Chaplin, actor and comedian, visits his British birth place after finding fame in Hollywood.

1922
Andrew Bonar Law (Conservative) becomes Prime Minister. The treasures of Tutankhamen are unearthed in Egypt.

1923
Stanley Baldwin (Conservative) becomes Prime Minister.

1924
James Ramsay MacDonald (Labour) becomes Prime Minister. Russian revolutionary Vladimir Lenin dies.

1926
Britain is paralysed by a General Strike.

1927
Charles Lindbergh flies non-stop and solo across the Atlantic.

1928
Alexander Fleming discovers penicillin. The first Disney cartoon with sound, *Steamboat Willie*, goes into cinemas.

1929
A woman joins the Cabinet for the first time after James Ramsay MacDonald is elected for a second term. Financial markets collapse after the Wall Street crash.

1930
Mahatma Gandhi begins a 300-mile walk across India in protest at Britain's proposed salt tax. Unemployment in Britain breaks the two million barrier.

1931
A coalition government takes over in Britain as the Labour administration fails.

1933
Hitler becomes Chancellor in Germany.

1935
Stanley Baldwin (Conservative) becomes Prime Minister again.

1936
George V dies and Edward VIII succeeds to the throne. However, upon his refusal to give up American divorcee Wallis Simpson, Edward abdicates. His younger brother, George VI, then succeeds to the throne. The BBC starts its new television service.

1937
Neville Chamberlain (Conservative) becomes Prime Minister. Japanese planes bomb Shanghai.

1939
General Franco is victorious in the Spanish Civil War. Outbreak of the Second World War. The film *The Wizard of Oz,* starring Judy Garland, is released.

1940
Sir Winston Churchill (Conservative) becomes Prime Minister. British forces are evacuated from Dunkirk as France falls to Germany.

1941
Germany invades Russia. The US naval base at Pearl Harbor is bombed by the Japanese, bringing America into the war.

1943
Allies land in Sicily to win a foothold in Europe. Italian dictator Mussolini falls from power.

1944
Normandy landings propel Allied troops back into France. Hitler's reprisal weapon, the pilotless V-1 bomb, begins raining down on London.

1945
Hitler commits suicide as Allied troops surround Berlin. The war in Europe ends in the spring. Clement Attlee (Labour) becomes Prime Minister. The first atomic bomb is dropped on Hiroshima.

1946
In the year Henry celebrates his 50th birthday, the captured leaders of Nazi Germany are sentenced at Nuremberg. The first conference linking smoking to cancer takes place at the University of Buffalo, in New York State.

1948
Mahatma Gandhi is assassinated just months after India gains independence from Britain. Russia blockades Berlin.

1950
Korean conflict begins.

1951
Sir Winston Churchill returns as Prime Minister.

1952
Upon the death of her father, George VI, Queen Elizabeth II succeeds to the throne.

1953
Russian dictator Joseph Stalin dies and is succeeded by Nikita Khrushchev. Mount Everest is conquered by New Zealander Edmund Hillary and Tenzing Norgay, a Nepalese Sherpa.

1954
Roger Bannister becomes the first man to run a mile in less than four minutes.

1955
Anthony Eden (Conservative) becomes Prime Minister.

1956
Egyptian leader Colonel Nasser seizes the Suez Canal from the French and British.

1957
Harold Macmillan (Conservative) becomes Prime Minister.

1961
Two months after Henry retires at the age of 65, East Germany begins building the Berlin Wall.

1963
US president John F. Kennedy is assassinated. Sir Alec Douglas-Home (Conservative) becomes Prime Minister.

1964
Harold Wilson (Labour) becomes Prime Minister.

1965
US planes bomb North Vietnam.

1966
Henry celebrates his 70th birthday. England wins the World Cup.

1969
Neil Armstrong becomes the first man to walk on the moon, at the pinnacle of the space race between the USA and the Soviet Union.

1970
Edward Heath (Conservative) becomes Prime Minister.

1971
Astronauts drive on the moon for the first time. The first heart and lung transplant is carried out by Christian Barnard in South Africa.

1973
The Government orders a three-day working week for two months to conserve electricity.

1974
Harold Wilson (Labour) returns as Prime Minister. Richard Nixon resigns as US President following the protracted Watergate affair, in which the White House bugged opposition offices.

1975
British people vote to join the European Common Market. The Vietnam war comes to an end: a defeat for the USA. Microsoft founded by Bill Gates.

1976
James Callaghan (Labour) becomes Prime Minister. Author Agatha Christie, born just six years before Henry, dies at the age of 85. Britain basks in a heatwave.

1977
Elvis Presley dies aged 42. Henry celebrates his 81st birthday.

1979
Margaret Thatcher (Conservative) becomes Prime Minister.

1981
Prince Charles marries Diana Spencer at St Paul's Cathedral.

1982
Falklands War is sparked by the Argentinian invasion of the islands in the South Atlantic. Within a few months, the war ends in victory for Britain.

1984
Police and coal miners battle on picket lines in South Yorkshire during the year-long Miners' Strike.

1985
Live Aid, two simultaneous concerts in Britain and America organised by Bob Geldof, raises £40 million for the starving in Africa.

1986
A nuclear reactor at Chernobyl power plant in the Soviet Union (now Ukraine) is destroyed by fire, accompanied by a massive radiation leak.

1988
The internet is opened to the commercial world.

1990
John Major (Conservative) becomes Prime Minister.

1996
In the year that Henry celebrates his 100th birthday, 16 children and a teacher are killed by a gunman at a primary school in Dunblane, Scotland. Madeleine Albright becomes the first female US Secretary of State. Dolly the sheep, the first cloned animal, is born in Scotland.

1997
Tony Blair (Labour) becomes Prime Minister.

2001
Two hijacked passenger aeroplanes fell the Twin Towers in New York.

2007
Gordon Brown (Labour) becomes Prime Minister.

2008
Henry celebrates his 112th birthday at RAF Cranwell in Lincolnshire.